HOW TO STUDY

How To Study: A Practical Guide

Second Edition

Francis Casey

First published 1985 by
THE MACMILLAN PRESS LTD
Houndmills, Basingstoke, Hampshire RG21 2XS
and London
Companies and representatives
throughout the world

ISBN 0–333–59788–5

A catalogue record for this book is available
from the British Library.

First edition reprinted six times
Second edition 1993
Reprinted 1994

Printed in Hong Kong

To
my mother
and to the memory of
my father

Contents

Acknowledgements

The author and publishers wish to thank the following who have kindly given permission for the use of copyright material:

The Controller, HMSO, for an extract from the *Annual Abstract of Statistics*.

Pitman Publishing Ltd, London, for an extract from *Plant and Animal Biology* by Vines and Rees.

Preface

It is not enough to study hard; you must learn how to study *efficiently*.

The aim of this book is to teach you the essentially simple techniques of personal organisation and study method, whether you are in the senior years of secondary school, at college or university, studying in adult education or following a correspondence course at home.

Students frequently under-achieve because of negative attitudes, poor planning and unawareness of basic approaches to the use of books, note making, essay writing and revision. *How To Study* offers detailed guidance in all of these areas, and many more.

The book is *practical* because it is understood that you do not have the time to pore over a lengthy volume, to concern yourself with theory or to work through a series of exercises related to the text. What you will find within is a wealth of commonsense advice – concisely and simply expressed – which you can begin to follow without delay.

My intention is that this book should represent a helpful and uncomplicated response to a very real need. For enabling me to identify the need, I am grateful to all of my students and pupils, past and present. For helping me to prepare this response, I am especially indebted to Andrew Berriman, for his committed and reliable assistance: to Jill Pinn, Andrew Manley and David Linsell, for their valuable contributions: to many other colleagues – too numerous to mention by name – for the wisdom and professional expertise on which I have been able to draw: to my wife, Gill, and children, Ben, Eleanor, Matthew and Jonathan, for their encouragement and unfailing support.

Francis Casey

1. First Principles

Although the opening remarks of this chapter are intended in the main for students in sixth forms and in full-time further and higher education, the section on 'Motivation' has much to say to students of *all* ages, no matter what their course or place of study may be.

The following points are central to your progress, and must be understood right from the beginning of your course:

(1) You have chosen to study further; it is not required by the state. Enrolling on a course will provide you with *opportunities* but will also impose *responsibilities*: to yourself, to develop your abilities as far as possible; to your fellow students, who have a right not to be deflected or interrupted by bad examples set by others; to those who teach you, who are making available to you the fruits of their hard work; in the case of sixth formers, to the rest of the school, which puts up with large group sizes so that you may enjoy small group tuition.

(2) You are facing an experience more challenging and rewarding than anything you have known so far:

(a) The work will be more demanding, but there will also be more scope for creativity, for the exercise of your own judgement, for individual decision-making. Many of you will have the benefit of small group tuition which gives students the opportunity to discuss ideas thoroughly. It is just as important to be able to express your ideas orally as to set them down in writing, and you should regard this as a skill to be consciously developed. Try to have the confidence to put forward your ideas and thoughts in

1

discussion, and you will help to make the experience more valuable and enjoyable for yourself and for the rest of the group.

(b) The pacing of your work is no longer imposed in detail from outside. *You* are now responsible for the organisation of your study pattern and work-load; frequently you will have several weeks in which to complete pieces of work. Often there will be essential preparatory work to be done, background reading to be undertaken.

(c) Private study periods in your timetable offer you an opportunity to get a lot of work done on site, where you have access to expert advice and works of reference. Sadly, for many people they become a profound waste of time. Sitting around doing nothing very much at all and kicking one's heels in a coffee-bar or common-room may have some appeal in September, but will soon become a millstone around your neck, making you fed up and depressed while the work piles up and the deadlines approach. *Don't let it happen to you.*

(d) You should now see teaching staff in a very different light: preferably not as figures of authority, but as senior partners in a shared activity. You must seek their help and advice openly, accept correction and guidance freely and participate fully in group work. Above all, you must take care to avoid the juvenile attitude according to which written work and prescribed reading are seen as counters in a game which you play *against* the staff, as things to be fiddled out of or delayed as long as possible. There is simply no place – or time – for such petty and damaging silliness.

(e) The main purpose of your course is not to *entertain* you, though it is obviously to be hoped that you will find the work rewarding. At all costs avoid the snap judgement of 'boring', which nearly always reveals more about the limitations and prejudices of the speaker than it does about the subject concerned.

(f) A spirit of co-operation with your fellow students is important; there is a need for constant discussion, planning and reading of each other's essays after they have been marked and returned. The stress should be on collaboration, not on competition.

(3) Motivation

The under-motivated student is one of the commonest species in the world of education. Typical habitats include common-rooms, coffee-bars, pubs and TV lounges, where the u-m-s may be observed putting off till tomorrow what really needed to be done yesterday. Notable characteristics include dullness of eye, general air of apathy and self-induced mood of boredom. By nature slow of movement, the u-m-s may occasionally be prodded into laborious action, but usually begrudges the effort. Survival rate: low.

Bear in mind the following:

(a) Unless you are outstandingly gifted, half-hearted effort will bring mediocre results.

(b) Your final grades will largely be the result of an extensive sequence of decisions and choices *made by you every day* during your course.

(c) If you feel your motivation weakening, consider the following points:

● It is quite likely that your performance will have a major bearing on your future career and life-style. There can be nothing so sad as regretting too late in life the mistakes made earlier on.

● Remind yourself of the higher education place, job or possible promotion that may depend on your performance.

● Your final grade may well be decided in part by the submission of a folder of coursework. If this is the case, there is no time to waste; the quality of your completed assignments *right from the word go* will play a central part in determining the level of your success – or failure.

● Remember that your grade will often be decided in part by the level of achievement of other students; you are not being assessed in isolation.

The main purpose is not to entertain you

● As well as these long-term objectives, set yourself a series of short-term aims: so much work to be done by Thursday evening, for instance. A sense of work achieved is a powerful motivator.

● Remember that time is precious – and limited. A 'two-year' full-time course in most institutions amounts in reality to a maximum of twenty-one months' work, while a 'one-year' course lasts for only nine months.

(d) Try seeking for the positive enjoyment in study: stretching yourself hard, finding inter-relatedness between topics, problem-solving, mastering difficult material. There is much in common with training for a sport – dabbling a toe in it will get you nowhere. Push yourself hard; make demands of yourself.

(e) Remember that you can always take an interest in a subject even if you do not readily like it. It may seem difficult to become absorbed in something that does not immediately appeal, but it is quite possible for a person to develop an interest in the detail of *anything* that he spends time on, whether it is studying rainfall in Asia, or painting a wall. Be prepared to, and you will find it happening. Be extra-vigorous in the area that appeals least; talk to others (including the staff!) who *do* like it; relate it to something you *do* find interesting. From childhood we are all fascinated by the fundamental inter-relatedness of things. The more you find out about a topic, the more you will perceive how one phenomenon links with another. This will please and intrigue you because man is naturally attracted by the discovery of such linkages.
It is clearly an advantage if you start with a definite liking for a subject, but even if this is absent, *you can develop an interest.*

(4) *Be quite clear about the commitment you are taking on.* Passes are not simply awarded as a token of your attendance or nominal membership of the course. Full-time students must be prepared to commit themselves to an average of approximately twenty hours of private study per week, in addition to 'taught time', as well as less pressurised work during the holidays. A realistic target for part-time and correspondence course students is likely to be somewhere in the region of ten to twelve hours per week.

(5) Whether you are fascinated or intimidated by computers, there is no avoiding the fact that information technology is likely to be a fundamental part of every student's working life. Information technology may be defined as the technology associated with the storage, retrieval, manipulation, communication and production of data by electronic means. The data may be textual, numerical, pictorial or aural, and the interaction facilitated by information technology may be between people and machines or between machines only. Your library may operate a computerised catalogue or offer access to vast banks of reference material . . . all at the touch of a few keys. The production, manipulation and revision of your own written work will be immensely enhanced – and much less time-consuming – if you can use a word-processor and/or desktop publishing programs. If you need to store, call up and rearrange information, you will find a data base invaluable. A spreadsheet program will enable you to record and present numerical/statistical information with supreme ease and efficiency. If your work involves a significant emphasis on visual/design elements, you will have access to an extensive range of programs in graphics and computer-aided design (CAD). Scientists and engineers will have a particular interest in programs which offer simulations, modelling and control technology applications. Students of music will be able to compose and revise multi-track scores with a computer rather than an orchestra. And so on. If you are already computer-literate, then the ever-expanding world of information technology is open to you, and the process of your studying will be greatly facilitated and liberated. If you are unfamiliar with computers but prepared to make the effort, you will never regret the extra initial input of time. What you must not do is hold yourself aloof from working with computers in the belief that if ignored, they will go away; at the very least, you will need to be prepared to sit down at a library keyboard so that your searching for reference material is not impeded.

(6) Try to start off with the right mental attitudes. This book should help you to approach your work in a well-balanced and sensibly organised way, to avoid obsessiveness as much as the last-minute panic to meet a deadline.

Have a realistic view of your own abilities, but do not underestimate yourself or you will find that you depress your standard accordingly.

Remember that if others in your group appear to 'out-class' you, this may not be because they are more *able* in grasping a point, but simply more *speedy* in grasping it. Take your time, ask for extra help if you need it, and you will get there in the end.

Don't bluff or conceal any problem that you may have, particularly in the early stages.

If you are troubled, TALK – to your subject teacher, tutor or any member of staff.

2.   *Early Practicalities*

(1) Course Structure

As early as possible, note down and familiarise yourself with details of the course in each of your subjects. You will almost certainly be given these details. If not, ask – and ask in the first week.

You need to know the following:

(a) The full title of the course and the syllabus number or code (if there is one).

(b) The topics and areas of study to be covered.

(c) Is there any optional element in the course? If so, how and when do you choose?

(d) How will you be assessed? Examination and/or coursework? Is there an oral? A practical? If a project or folder of coursework is to be prepared, what is the deadline? Are there any restrictions on the number of word-processed coursework assignments that may be submitted?

(e) How many examination papers? How long are they? Which examining board? How can you get hold of past papers?

(f) If at any time you have been designated as having special educational needs (dyslexia, moderate learning difficulties etc.), check whether you are entitled to any dispensations in the exam situation; these could include such provision as an extra allocation of time or a tape-recorded version of the examination paper.

(g) Approximate dates of trial, intermediate and final examinations.

(h) How often will you be set work? How long should the preparation and writing up take?

When you have learned the answers to all of these questions, set out the details in a neat fact-sheet and place it in the front of the appropriate subject file (see below). This will give you, right from the beginning, a sense of clarity about your aim, your eventual destination, and an awareness of what is to be required of you.

(2) Equipment

Your attitude here is vitally important. Being prepared to equip yourself properly symbolises your willingness to commit yourself to the work, to make a go of things; it also treats you to the very real pleasure of gathering significant and new things about you as you make a fresh start on a new phase of your life.

You will need:

(a) Ring-binders: one for each subject. These to be kept at home for your notes, essays and duplicated copies to be inserted and stored as they come to hand.

(b) A 'transit' file: for carrying papers to and fro. NOT a permanent resting place, merely a means of transport.

(c) Your own supply of A4 file paper: for obvious reasons, and to relieve you of the necessity to traipse around picking up the odd sheet of paper here and there.

(d) A hole-punch and ring-reinforcements: to enable you to file anything as appropriate in your ring-binders and to avoid damage to the sheets in use.

(e) Coloured pens and pencils: *vital* for good note-taking and rearrangements (see Chapter 6).

(f) A small stapler: to enable you to add extra sheets efficiently and in the correct place to something already written.

(g) A study schedule pad: an absolute necessity, to be explained in the next chapter.

(h) Small, cheap jotters: for noting brief details of work set, points to be checked, reminders and so on. *Do not use your files for this*.

(i) Vocabulary note-book: to be explained in Chapter 4.

(j) Specialist equipment: check with teaching staff the necessity for such things as calculators, instruments and other specific items.

(k) The last chapter referred to the importance of students feeling at ease with the many uses of information technology. You will usually have access to the required computer facilities at school/ college, but it will be a great advantage – though not a necessity – if you have your own computer at home. Most of the leading makes will give you the operational scope that you need, but you should try to ensure that your system at home is compatible with the installation at school/college; this will ensure that disks and software are interchangeable and that work may be proceeded with in either place. For preference, you should probably aim to acquire a PC (personal computer) which is IBM compatible.

(l) Reference books: you should always carry with you an easily portable dictionary. At home you should have a good, up-to-date single-volume dictionary. Particularly recommended is the *Chambers Twentieth Century*. A thesaurus is also useful; if you don't know what it is, find out (see Appendix 2). It will enrich your style and could alter your whole attitude to writing.

You will also need a general work of reference for checking a wide range of background facts and essential information. Macmillan publish a splendidly authoritative and comprehensive single-volume encyclopaedia.

Check with individual subject staff whether they recommend purchase of specialist works of reference.

You will be expected to buy some books during the course. Seek for the pleasure in building up a small library of your own, possibly with your own personalised 'Ex libris' bookplates. Appendix 1 should prove helpful in this connection.

If you have scorned any of the above suggestions, take time out to examine your attitudes and expectations. The blotchy ball-pen and dog-eared folder syndrome all too often reflects a casual and flippant attitude which could undermine you from the outset.

3. How to Plan Your Study

If you do not manage your work-load in a pre-planned and structured way, a number of the following statements made by students will soon be applying to you:

'I sit and gaze at books for hours, but I get very little done.'
'I can't get the balance right; I find any excuse to put it off.'
'It's difficult to cope with all the reading I'm supposed to do.'
'Concentration is my problem; I can't settle to anything for very long.'
'There doesn't seem to be enough time.'
'I just can't meet the deadlines; the work keeps piling up.'

If you do adopt – and maintain – a planned approach, you *will* keep on top of the work, meet your deadlines and *still* have more than enough time left for relaxation and enjoyment. Most important of all, you will benefit from a sense of achievement which will strengthen your confidence in the future and increase your appetite for work.

(1) There are Two Elements to Good Planning

(a) The first step is to make regular and complete lists of things to be done. Draw up a list for each week, preferably at the same time – say Sunday evening – as you look ahead and see what is to be done in the next seven-day cycle. Details for this list will come from your rough note-book.

Types of work appearing in your list could include the following:

(i) Preliminary reading on a topic about to be covered; ask for advance notice.

(ii) Preparatory collection of material and rough work for an essay or other written piece.

(iii) Final 'write-up' of the above.

(iv) Re-reading (and perhaps re-writing and amplifying) of notes, which are usually best taken in rough first of all, then written up later. This acts as a first stage of revision, and prevents you from writing notes that you do not understand. If you are uncertain about some point in your notes, ask about it without delay. Make this a daily habit; it need take only a very short time, but is invaluable for consolidating and fixing in the mind.

(v) Regular reviews of material already covered (see Chapter 10).

(vi) General background reading.

(b) The next step is to compile a chart for the week, with each day sub-divided into a number of sessions. Base the length of the sessions on the duration of your classes or lectures, as this will be a unit familiar to you, and already part of your work rhythm.

You will find illustrated a sample 'study schedule sheet' based on a one-hour period structure. Copy this pattern carefully onto a sheet of A4 paper, altering the units as required, then take enough photocopies – one per week – to cover an academic year. Bind these together, and you will have a useful study schedule pad which will be at the very centre of your planning and personal organisation.

The principle is that when you have 'blocked out' on the sheet your 'taught time' for the week, together with a reasonable 'allowance' for recreation and relaxation, you will see *exactly* how much

Week beginning:

	Mon	Tues	Wed	Thur	Fri	Sat	Sun
P.1							
P.2							
P.3							
P.4							
P.5							
4.00–5.00							
5.00–6.00							
6.00–7.00							
7.00–8.00							
8.00–9.00							
9.00–10.00							

Tasks for the week:
(include reading and rough work, as well as final writing up. Insert date deadline after each item.)

_____

_____

_____

_____

_____

_____

_____

time is available to you – divided into suitable sessions – to cover the work in hand.

If you are a full-time student, it has already been pointed out that you should expect to devote at least twenty hours of your own time each week to independent study, but you will be surprised at the ease with which your schedule for the week can accommodate this – as long as you stick to it. All you have to do is:

(i)   Settle a regular time each week when you will draw up your schedule.

(ii) List at the side of the sheet *all* of the things you have to do, adding details of deadlines where appropriate.

(iii) 'Block-out' your taught time and social commitments.

(iv) Transfer the items from the 'things to do' list into suitable time blocks in your schedule. Of course some of your tasks, for example an essay, will need more than one time block. It may be worthwhile to leave some unallocated time each day to 'mop up' unfinished tasks.

The very act of doing this regularly will give you a sense of confidence *in advance* that you are going to be able to manage a particular week's work-load, rather than worry about it as an over-whelming burden in prospect.

Note

● When compiling your schedule for the week ahead, check back to last week's to see if there was anything you failed to complete. If so, add it to this week's list.

● If, as you go through the week you have planned, you fail to complete a particular task in the time you have allocated, give it a further allocation of time later in the week.

● In your list of things to do, a simple code of single (*) or double (**) asterisks will serve to indicate the relative urgency of particular tasks.

● The sample schedule sheet indicates that you should stop work by 10.00 p.m. at the latest; the need for this will vary from one person to another, but as a general rule, it is counter-productive to work too late.

● If you are doing a solid evening's work (perhaps from 7.00–10.00) take short, five-minute breaks between the hour-long sessions. Beware, however, the dangers of being diverted.

● In such a three-hour session, go for variety, if this is at all possible. For example:
7.00 – 8.00:   Imagery in *King Lear* – check and re-write notes.
8.00 – 9.00:   Final write-up of essay on 'Control of Money Supply'.
9.00 – 10.00: Background reading on early history of Marxism.

● In each study session, no matter what the length, *begin work straightaway*, perhaps by briefly looking over what you last did on this topic, or by making a list of checkpoints as they occur to you. This will help you to overcome the 'arm's length syndrome' in which students sit down but fail to get started.

● At the end of each study session, review briefly what you have covered (see Chapter 10).

● The sample schedule sheet divides the week into seventy-seven usable time-slots; even after subtracting approximately twenty of these for taught time, as many as you need for eating and travel and your allocation of time for personal recreation, you will still have *more than enough* to accommodate your twenty hours of study time.

● Your aim must be to establish a balanced and sensible spread of study periods. Try above all to avoid bouts of frenzied activity interspersed with periods of comparative idleness.

● If, as a full-time student, certain sessions of your week are regularly devoted to some non-academic activity such as training for a sport or paid employment, then other sessions

Beware the dangers of being diverted

(for example four nights a week and two sessions on Sunday) should be devoted equally regularly to academic work. You should beware the very real danger of spending too much time on a part-time job at the expense of your studies. There is a close correlation between such commitments and poor examination results. You should never spend more than one night in the week and one day at the weekend on such activities, and preferably less. Indeed, it is often financially short-sighted to sacrifice good examination results (which can lead to real financial reward in the future) for short-term earnings. You should question your life-style if you feel it is vitally necessary to spend several evenings and a weekend earning money. The demands of a full academic work-load are such that to adopt this course of action is tantamount to inevitable under-performance in coursework and examinations.

(2) Where to Study

(a) *On Site*

Avoid common-rooms and anywhere conversation is likely. Use the library if at all possible; works of reference are at hand, and the atmosphere of silence is likely to be conducive to concentration. Respect this atmosphere by working in silence, so as not to disturb others around you. University and public libraries insist on this rule. Your line of vision is important; try to avoid positions which give you a view of the whole room or large numbers of other people.

(b) *At Home*

You should *never* work where other people are sitting around and chatting or where the TV is on. Avoid also the temptation to work while stretched out on bed or settee.

Ideally, you should set aside a place which will be used only by you (the corner of your bedroom will be fine), and which you can turn into a permanent study area. You will need the following:

- A flat work-surface at the right height (750mm). You ought to be able to leave books and papers out for as long as you wish, without always having to clear them away. All materials and instruments should be close at hand.

- If you have a PC (personal computer), this should be kept ready for immediate use and preferably installed nearby. It certainly should not occupy the work surface used for conventional work by hand.

- A suitable chair.

- A desk-lamp, preferably one with a clearly-defined cone of light which will focus your attention.

- Bookshelves.

- A wall-mounted pin-board on which to display charts, diagrams and last-minute reminders.

- A clock.

- Reasonable warmth and ventilation.

- As little noise as possible – most chemists stock a cheap and useful line in ear-plugs!

In arranging both your weekly schedule and your home study area, aim from the start for a professional and 'no-nonsense' approach.

4. *Reading*

We would all claim to be able to read, but the truth is that few people read efficiently. The single word 'reading' is itself misleadingly simple, for *there are many different techniques of reading* required of us according to the task in hand: scanning a telephone directory, checking a recipe, flicking through a book to see if it is useful, 'reading' a complex mathematical formula, studying a chapter of Jane Austen, enjoying a le Carré spy novel. All of these call for a different reading approach, but most people only have one: slow, one-paced and rather ponderous. This will clearly be a major drawback to you when you have so much reading to get through.

(1) You Need the Following Skills

(a) *Reading to evaluate*: to find out rapidly whether a book, publication or article is of any use to you, adopt the following approaches:

(i)   Check foreword/preface/introduction – there should be an indication here of the type and scope of the content. Is this really what you want?

(ii)   Is the author an authority? How many other similar or related books has he written? Check the list of his publications at the front or back, together with any biographical detail.

(iii) Check the date of publication – it is possible that the information may be out of date. You may need to seek a more recent edition.

(iv) Does it have footnotes, an index, a bibliography? If not, it may be an indication of a rather superficial approach.

(b) *Skim reading*: to gain rapidly a general idea of the content of a book, examine briefly the following:

(i) Table of contents, which will give chapter headings and, possibly, sub-headings.

(ii) The index: pay particular attention to index entries which show several pages devoted to a particular subject, for this will show you the author's main concerns and where the emphasis comes.

(iii) Check briefly any sub-headings in the body of the text.

(iv) Look at first and last sentences of chapters and first and last sentences of long paragraphs.

(c) *Reading to study*: a technique – perhaps the only one – which you already know well. You may have been set a book to study, or perhaps your evaluation or skim reading has led you to a chapter worth knowing thoroughly. In any case, we are dealing here with slow and repetitive reading, the aim being to master entirely the main ideas, facts and arguments of the writer. *Skim read it first*, perhaps lightly marking in pencil certain sections or important ideas to which you will return when you have finished your first reading; jot down what you consider to be the chief issues or concerns, then read again slowly and carefully, taking particular care over difficult ideas. The aim is to abstract the key points of detail, concepts, lines of argument and so on.

(d) *Word-by-word reading*: this type of slow and perceptive reading is probably most often called for in complex scientific or mathematical writing, or perhaps in seeking to appreciate the full beauty and significance of a poem or other piece of literature.

(2) Try to Adopt a Challenging and Enquiring Attitude to Your Reading

Ask yourself why you are reading a particular book and what you hope to gain from it. Engage in a kind of dialogue with the book, as if it is a person with whom you are holding a discussion. Make judgements about what is written; because it is in print does not mean that it must be regarded as gospel truth and totally objective. Is there anything wrong with the author's views and attitudes? Has he fully supported his arguments? Could you refute them? What evidence would you bring forth to do so? Is he biased?

(3) Speed Reading

There has been a considerable vogue for speed reading in recent years, and there is no doubt that increasing your reading speed will enable you to cope more efficiently with your work-load – and to enjoy more leisure reading. Politicians, civil servants and journalists frequently take courses in speed reading to help them manage the huge quantity of written material that they must deal with.

Most people read at a speed of 300–400 words per minute; a speed well below this will hamper you in your work, and certainly needs to be improved upon.

You may be interested in the following approaches, which are central to the teaching of faster and more efficient reading:

(a) Time reduction: take any not very important book that you may be reading, establish the approximate number of words per page, and measure *exactly* the time taken to read, say four pages. Attempt to reduce this in methodical fashion with each subsequent block of four pages, though obviously you must not gain speed at the expense of understanding. Establish a routine of 'training sessions' with the emphasis on time reduction. Keep a note of your times, which are best recorded in terms of words per minute.

(b) The real secret of rapid reading is to train your eyes to *see more*. When most people read, they proceed laboriously through very short units of words/half-words/letters. Try to achieve an improvement by training your eyes to see larger word-blocks, by moving your eyes down the centre of the page or by adopting a swift zig-zag eye movement.

You need to reduce the number of 'eye fixations' that you make in each line. In the sentence 'Ben drove to the garage to fill up with petrol' an efficient reader would be likely to make the following fixations:

    1   2

'Ben drove to the garage to fill up with petrol.'

A slow reader would make far more visual fixations or 'attention pauses' as follows:

   1   2   3   4   5

'Ben drove to the garage to fill up with petrol.'

(c) Concentrate on essential ideas and the main substance; avoid pondering too long on minor issues.

(d) When reading rapidly, try to avoid what teachers of reading call 'regression', that is looking back over a sentence, or part of a sentence, that has been read.

(e) Avoid 'vocalisation', which is the habit of saying the words to yourself, even mentally.

If you wish to adopt a structured and serious approach to boosting your reading speed, try the following books:

Speed Reading – Tony Buzan (Sphere 1971)
Read Better, Read Faster – de Leeuw (Penguin Books 1969).

If you work hard at this, you should eventually be able to increase your speed to somewhere in the region of 500 words per minute.

(4) Leisure Reading

You should regularly read for pleasure – don't let reading become merely an academic chore. If you care about the sort of personality you will ultimately become, take care to 'feed' it well with a diet of diverse recreational reading. This will increase your stock of ideas, enable you to enlarge your general knowledge, acquire a greater understanding of man and his world – and have a lot of fun. Ideally your coursework reading and leisure reading should cross-fertilise and enrich each other.

Your choice of private reading is your affair, but if you would like some guidance, you will find in Appendix 1 a list of recommended books. Dip in and enjoy yourself.

Another form of reading which should be part of your programme – and thus built into your schedule – has to do with newspapers and periodicals. You ought to be attuning yourself to serious thought and preoccupations by regular reading from one or more of the 'quality' newspapers and magazines listed in Appendix 3. You will find it enormously beneficial to set aside an hour or two per week for private reading of sophisticated journalism. Do not restrict yourself to news features and sport. Read arts reviews and other critical pieces; these will undoubtedly help to refine your own style in the fundamentally similar sorts of written work that you have to produce as part of your course.

(5) Vocabulary Building

Consider the following words:

hypothesis	abhorrent	appraise
increment	arbitrary	autonomous
quasi-	fastidious	dichotomy
spontaneous	incongruous	elucidate
subjective/objective	moribund	proscribe
transient	soporific	protagonist

accession	composite
cede	arbitration
cessation	versatility
devolution	differentials
indemnity	demarcation
reparation	depleted

How many of these works could *you* define precisely? The point is important, for all of the words were taken from questions set in five recent examinations – in arts, science and vocational subjects – designed for the sixteen to eighteen age range.

There is nothing special about the papers in question; they were chosen at random. The samples shown should serve, therefore, to emphasise an issue of basic significance: quite bluntly, you are not likely to flourish in your answers if you do not understand some of the words in the questions!

You should now be regarding the expansion of your vocabulary as an issue of prime importance. Think back to the 'shopping list' of new equipment and you will recall the need for vocabulary note-books – certainly more than one if you are going to be serious about it. Keep your rough jotter with you whenever you are reading; scribble down any word you do not understand, but generally wait until you have collected several before having a 'looking up' session. Transfer the definitions to your vocabulary note-book, with – if possible – sample sentences to show usage. Do not be afraid to ask for help with definitions and sample sentences. Be a word collector!

Do not then allow your vocabulary note-book to become a graveyard of dead definitions. Convert your new words from the passive to the active. USE them, even at the risk of occasional inaccuracy.

We often hear of somebody having a strong or forceful personality; when stripped of inessentials, this usually means that he is articulate, never at a loss for words, always able to speak fluently. A wide and flexible *active* vocabulary is vital if you are to express yourself precisely, to capture fine shades of meaning and to avoid irritating cliches and slang. If your vocabulary is stunted and immature so – inevitably – will be the quality of your thought and expression.

(6) Abbreviations

You must be familiar with the following words and abbreviations, which you will find frequently in the text and/or index of many books:

c.   (circa) about: usually with a date, to show that it is only approximate. For example: c.930.

cf.   (confer) compare.

do.   (ditto) the same.

e.g.   (exempli gratia) for example.

esp.   especially.

et al.   (et alii, aliae, or alia) and others: to save writing out a whole list of names. For example: Hatten et al.

et seq.   (et sequens) and the following. For example: p. 36 et seq.

f./ff   following. For example: 8f. = page 8 and the following page. 8ff. = page 8 and the following pages.

ibid   (ibidem) in the same place: used in an index to show that the reference in question comes from the book previously mentioned.

i.e.   (id est) that is.

inf.   (infra) below: refers to a section still to come.

loc.cit. (loco citato) at the place quoted: used in an index to show that the reference in question comes from the same place in a book as the previous one.

op.cit.   (opere citato) from the work quoted: used in an index.

p./pp.   page/pages.

passim   in many places: often found in an index, to indicate that there are many references to a particular person or topic, perhaps too many to list.

q.v.   (quod vide) literally 'which see'; look up this point or topic elsewhere in this book. For example: q.v. p. 32.

sic   thus. Used when you wish to quote a word or extract, written by somebody else, which contains a mistake or inaccuracy. It is a way of indicating that it is not *your* mistake. For example: The parents wrote a note saying that the boy was too fritened (sic) to come to school.

supra   above: in the part of the book or chapter already dealt with.

viz   (videlicet) namely, that is to say.

5. *Using Libraries*

'Knowledge is of two kinds. We know a subject ourselves, or we know where we can find information upon it.' [Dr Samuel Johnson]

It is crucially important for you to acquire confidence and skill in using libraries. Far too many students go through their whole education without achieving this, tending to regard libraries at best as quiet places for essay writing, with no more than occasional use of the book-stock. Many appear in some way to be intimidated or daunted by the vast array of material, feeling that they somehow lack the sophistication to turn these huge resources to their own advantage.

The first point to establish, therefore, is that using a library properly and to the full is essentially a matter of a few simple techniques which will enable you to extract the material you require.

(1) Most public and general libraries are divided into three main areas – fiction, non-fiction and reference. They may all be contained in one room, or each may occupy a separate room or floor of a building, depending on the size of the library and the space available. *Fiction* is the term used to describe novels and stories of the imagination, both classics and popular pleasure reading. *Non-fiction* describes technical and factual works, and books which cover events and things that exist in reality. There are, of course, some areas of investigation, for example psychic phenomena and UFOs, where 'existence' is uncertain, but for the purposes of library arrangement, these areas are allocated space within the non-fiction section. *Reference* books are simply non-fiction books of a kind

Many appear to be daunted

which cannot be borrowed from the library and must therefore be consulted on the premises, usually in a reading-room set aside for this purpose. Any person may use any public reference library.

(2) Library Arrangement

Fiction is usually arranged in alphabetical sequence of the author's surname, for example Richard Adams under 'A' and Jack Higgins under 'H'. Some libraries divide their fiction into categories, and shelve all the crime stories in one block and all the science fiction in another, and so on. Most, however, do not have the space to do this, and many use either coloured tags or letter codes on the spines of the books to denote the type of story.

Non-fiction and *reference* books are arranged *in subject groups*. The system used by most libraries in many countries is an American one, developed by a man called Melvil Dewey (1851–1931). It is a system which allocates a number between 1 and 999 to each subject, grouping similar subjects together as far as is possible, and which by the use of decimals and various mnemonic devices is capable of almost infinite expansion. Although by no means perfect, no other system has yet surpassed it. It is known as the Dewey Decimal Classification System. Below is a guide to the main divisions of the system:

First Summary
000 – 099	Generalities
100 – 199	Philosophy and related disciplines
200 – 299	Religion
300 – 399	The social sciences
400 – 499	Languages
500 – 599	Pure sciences
600 – 699	Applied sciences (technology)
700 – 799	Fine arts
800 – 899	Literature
900 – 999	Geography, biography and history

These ten main 'hundreds' are further divided into 'tens' and some of these are as follows:

Second Summary

100	Philosophy	600	Technology
110	Metaphysics	610	Medicine
120	Man and knowledge	620	Engineering
130	Parapsychology	630	Agriculture
140	Specific philosophies	640	Domestic sciences
150	Psychology	650	Managerial sciences
160	Logic	660	Chemical and related . . .
170	Ethics	670	Manufactures
180	Ancient philosophy	680	Crafts & miscellaneous
190	Modern philosophy	690	Building sciences

From here, the system further sub-divides into 'units' for greater detail:

Third Summary

660	Chemical and related technologies
661	Industrial chemicals
662	Explosives, fuels, related products
663	Beverage technology
664	Food technology
665	Industrial oils, fats, waxes, gases
666	Ceramic and allied technologies
667	Cleaning, colour and related technology
668	Other organic products
669	Metallurgy

With the introduction of decimal points after the three-figure number, even further detail is possible:

664	Food technology
664.1	Sugars, syrups and derived products
664.2	Starches and jellying agents

664.3	Fats and oils
664.4	Food salts
664.5	Other flavouring aids
664.6	Special purpose foods and aids
664.7	Grains, other seeds, their derived products
664.8	Fruits and vegetables
664.9	Meats and allied foods

Not all books can be fitted neatly into one category. In this instance, normal practice is to put the book into the number of the major topic covered, or into the first two adjacent numbers where this is applicable. Roughly speaking, the longer the Dewey number, the more detailed the text.

Mnemonics are used in the system, the most useful of which is that which refers to Britain. It is the number used for British geography and history, that is 942. There is a numeric link between the two subjects in that British geography = 914.2 and British history = 942. The history number can then be added to most other subject numbers to imply that the book deals with the British aspect of the subject, for example:

330	=	Economics
330.9	=	Economic history
330.942	=	British economic history

This numeric link applies in similar fashion to other countries. A further example:

914.7	=	Russian geography
947	=	Russian history
330.947	=	Russian economic history

All non-fiction and reference books are marked with their correct subject numbers on the spines of the books. They are then filed on the shelves in number order, which has the effect of bringing together all the books on each particular subject – to the great advantage of the reader. You will see that it is a very precise, accurate and detailed system, and it lends itself to two methods of approach. If you know exactly which book you want, you can consult the catalogue and be directed to its precise place on the shelf; if you want information on a subject – but the source is unimportant – you can look up the subject number in the catalogue and be directed to the correct area for your search.

(3) Catalogues

Catalogues come in three major forms – the card catalogue, the book catalogue and the computer terminal. Entries in each category will be similar, although some will be more detailed than others. The average card catalogue entry will look something like the examples below. Fiction entries are usually less detailed than those for non-fiction, for reasons which will become obvious.

NON-FICTION

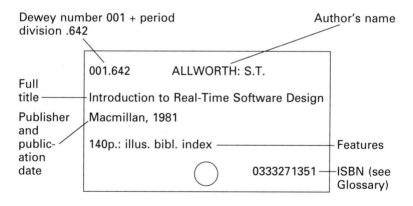

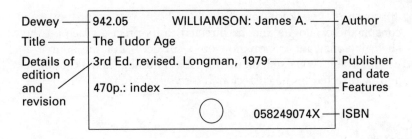

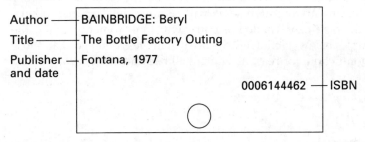

NOTE: No Dewey number for fiction.

Catalogues usually have more than one sequence. Fiction catalogues will have entries under author (by surname alphabetically), title (omitting definite and indefinite articles), and sometimes a classified list by type of story. The non-fiction catalogue will have an entry under the author's surname and sometimes the title, although this is not usual. The second entry is usually made under the Dewey number in a numeric sequence. This is so that a reader, having found the Dewey number he requires, can check through the total library stock on that subject and see all the resources available, be they reference books, books on loan at present, books kept in odd places for various reasons and so on. The third sequence which most libraries will have is the *Subject Index*. These are entries in alphabetical order which carry only the subject name and the appropriate Dewey number. If you were to look up *Plastics*, for instance, you would probably find a card like this:

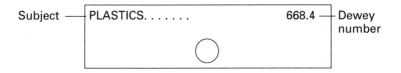

These cards are sometimes filed separately, sometimes in alphabetical sequence with the authors.

The best computerised catalogues will combine simplicity of use with a range of easily-accessed information. Most systems will carry out rapid subject or author searches in order to identify titles relevant to your area of interest. They are also likely to be able to indicate which books are in the library and which are out on loan, and will provide a host of other useful services. You don't need to be a computer expert in order to benefit from these resources. Almost all catalogues – whether card or computer – have instructions for use conveniently placed, but any librarian will be pleased to help should the need arise.

(4) Reference Books

You will frequently need to use reference books, and should find the following information useful.

There are general reference works such as encyclopaedias, which cover many subjects and are usually arranged alphabetically. The most famous and authoritative of the multi-volume general encyclopaedias is still 'The Encyclopaedia Britannica', now sub-divided into three sections (see Appendix 2). There are also encyclopaedias on many specialist subjects, such as encyclopaedias of sport, history, art, geology and so on. Dictionaries of all languages are also available, and here again it is possible to find dictionaries of science, fine arts, medicine, meteorology and many others. The Penguin dictionaries are fine examples of these. Several current atlases provide tables of social and general interest as well as maps, and gazetteers may cover the whole world or small regions. There are many fine reference books on almost every subject imaginable.

In Appendix 2 you will find listed a small selection of some of the better known general and specialist works of reference.

Frequently your reference work will require you to examine such material as newspapers, periodicals and journals. Traditionally, back copies have been bound for reference use, but increasingly the pages are reduced to microfilm format and need to be scanned with a special viewer. Such machines are very user-friendly and the library assistants will be glad to guide you.

As in the construction and use of catalogues, computerisation in the library has also begun to transform the reference section. Books will never go out of fashion, but it is true that many large dictionaries, encyclopaedias and directories of resources – as well as back copies of authoritative newspapers – are now digitally stored on compact disc (CD–Rom), ready to be called on to the display screen by a few touches on the keyboard. This mode of storage and access is expanding constantly and the wise student will wish to become, and remain, aware of what is available to him.

(5) To conclude, there follows a list of the information you need in order to make the fullest and most efficient use of your library:

(a) Location of catalogues.

(b) Number and types of catalogues.

(c) Is there a non-fiction subject index in the catalogue?

(d) Location (that is, Dewey number) of books on your subject areas.

(e) Location of reference section.

(f) Reference books on your subject areas.

(g) Maximum number of books to be borrowed. Period of loan.

(h) Does the library have the books on your reading lists?

(i) Location of bound (or microfilmed) periodicals and journals. Are they indexed?

(j) Location of current periodicals.

(k) Periodicals in your subject areas.

(l) Is there a local studies collection of books, newspapers and pictures concerning your district?

(m) Availability of: Maps, plans, land surveys, records and tapes of music, speech, drama, music scores, play sets for reading and production.

(n) Availability of microfilm viewers.

(o) Facilities for photocopying.

Remember that one of the most valuable resources in a library is the trained librarian. If you are not sure, ask for help.

6. *Notes*

Efficient note-taking is a skill that must be acquired if you are to manage your work-load satisfactorily and do full justice to your ability. The taking of notes forces you to concentrate on the matter in hand, to identify and understand the chief points. It keeps you *active* while learning. Notes also represent a good deal of the written work upon which you will depend for revision, as well as some of the raw material that you will need in preparing to write essays and other coursework assignments.

(1) You are likely to take notes from two main sources:

(a) *Books, articles, documents*

Adopt the following procedure:

(i)   Check that the book is appropriate to your needs and generally considered to be of value (see Chapter 4).

(ii)   Take a careful note of the title, author and date. These details should appear at the head of your page of notes.

(iii) Skim read (see Chapter 4) to find the most valuable sections; look at the contents, introduction, conclusion, index.

(iv)   Having identified a chapter or section on which you wish to take notes, *read it through in full before taking any notes*; this will enable you to see the overall structure and identify the chief points.

(v)   Make notes during the second reading.

(vi)   Use *your own words* (unless quoting) as far as possible. Your notes should represent your understanding of the material, rather than your skill in copying.

(vii)   Be *brief*; avoid 'whole sentence' notes (unless quoting). Seek out and use *keywords and phrases*.

(viii) *Never* underline or make notes in a book that does not belong to you. Even if the book is yours, underlining and brief margin comments are a very poor second best to making your own notes on paper.

(b) *Lessons, lectures, seminars*

(i)   The teacher/lecturer will probably be working from pre-structured notes already arranged in sections.

(ii)   In view of this, listen for 'sign-post' words, phrases or gestures which indicate the divisions between the different stages in his material.

(iii)   Try as far as possible to rephrase his words.

(iv)   *Identify the key points*; do not attempt to get down everything that is said.

(v)   If you do not understand or if you fall behind or miss a point, ASK – either for clarification or repetition.

(vi)   *As soon as possible* after the lesson or lecture, rework your notes. Never be satisfied with them in their original form. Re-read, filling in any gaps, clarifying any uncertainties, adding extra material. Re-write them if you have time or if they strike you as being at all inadequate. If you are not re-writing, at the very least go through your notes with coloured pens, underlining headings and sub-section titles, circling or boxing particularly important names, facts, details.

    This second phase of the note-taking process is crucial: it roots the subject matter more firmly in your mind, and makes your notes much easier to use for essays and revision.

(2) Materials

Your start-of-course shopping list referred to ring-binders, coloured pens and lots of file paper. Their usefulness should by now be clear to you. The ring-binders in particular offer flexibility of storage. You can store notes, hand-outs and photocopies as you will and rearrange them if necessary. Do keep your main binders (one or more for each subject) safely at home, carrying around with you only a blank pad and/or your 'transit' file.

(3) Layout

If your notes are to be at all useful for revision and preparation for written assignments, they must be *methodically structured and well set out*. The points which follow represent an ideal, but you should always aim to implement them, even under the pressure of hurried note-taking:

(a) *Legibility* is crucial. If your notes are at all scrawled or unclear, they *must* be re-written. Badly written, ugly or untidy notes are a powerful disincentive when the time comes to use them.

(b) *'White space'* is vitally important. You must not write from margin to right-hand edge or from top to bottom of the page, or you will be left with an intimidating block of verbiage which denies future flexibility of use. Blank space around and between lines is important *visually* as it allows you more easily to focus on important points. It is also important *practically* because it allows you to add further material later on. It is better to use wide-lined paper.

(c) *One side only*. Although it may appear extravagant, you will be able to use your notes far more easily and with less risk of

Ring-binders offer flexibility of storage

confusion and of 'losing the thread' if you use only one side of the paper.

(d) *Colour* is very useful. It helps to draw the attention to section divisions, important headings and so on, and may also be used to circle or box a particularly important fact, detail, date or name in the body of the notes. As indicated in the case of 'white space', it is worth using every available tactic to fix your notes vividly in the mind.

(e) *Main and side headings* are useful techniques of dividing the material up into 'digestible' sections, as well as indicating the chief stages in the development of the theme or line of thought. When you revise, if you can remember the actual headings in sequence, the details under each heading will be absorbed with less difficulty. *Number the side-headings* efficiently and accurately. Main sections, sub-sections and further sub-divisions should be designated in a clearly defined way. Use a combination of large roman numerals (I, II, III, IV), capital letters (A, B, C, D), arabic numerals (1, 2, 3, 4), lower-case letters (a, b, c, d) and small roman numerals (i, ii, iii, iv). Once you have decided on your system of numbering and lettering for main sections and sub-sections, *stick to it*. Also, remember to number the sheets of your notes, to maintain efficient ordering and in case of major catastrophe if your file falls open.

(f) *Indentation* (moving in from the margin before starting to write) is a very useful visual tactic to indicate that a significant new stage is beginning. If you are indenting, do so *emphatically*.

(g) *Diagrams and drawings* should be used wherever possible; they can be visualised more clearly in the mind than written prose.

(h) *Abbreviations* are a significant help in speedy note-taking. Decide on a system – inventing your own abbreviations if you wish – but once you have decided, be consistent. Apart from abbreviated forms of words, the following are some of the more common abbreviations:

>	is greater than
<	is less than
∴	therefore
∵	because
=	equals
c.f.	compare, or remember in this context
≠	does not equal, is different from
→	leads to, led to, caused
←	is caused by, depends on

(i) *'Linear'* or sequential listing is the more traditional and widely favoured method of setting down notes, though some people favour the patterned or diagrammatic approach. Supporters of the latter claim that is is more visually memorable, and that it makes relationships more clear. Both techniques are illustrated at the end of the chapter; choice between the two is essentially a matter of personal preference, though scientific and technical notes are often better presented in diagrammatic form.

(4) Faults to Avoid

Consider, and do your best to avoid, the following common faults:

(a) *General layout*

(i)   Unsuitable or varied paper size; standardise on A4.

(ii) Pages too cramped and crowded; this makes it difficult to gain 'visual access' to the notes.

(iii) Different topics jumbled together.

(iv) Poor handwriting.

(b) *Note structure*

(i)   Inadequate or non-existent labelling at the top of the page.

(ii) Not enough 'white space'.

(iii) Insufficient number of headings, sub-headings, indentations. You should *never* have more than one third of a page of notes without a heading or sub-heading.

(iv) Difficult to perceive organisation and linking of stages and ideas.

(c) *Content and wording*

(i)   Main points omitted.

(ii) Too much unnecessary detail.

(iii) Too 'wordy'.

(iv) Unclear or vague wording.

(v)   Too much in the words of the original, not enough in your own.

(5) Filing

(a) Keep all of your notes on any one topic together.

(b) Beware the danger of filing photocopies ad nauseam without carefully reading and understanding them first.

(c) Number the pages and establish an index or contents page in your storage file.

(d) For reasons of security, *never* carry around your main storage files.

(6) Sample Notes

Read the following passage carefully and then examine how it can be reduced to note form in traditional 'linear' fashion and then in patterned style:

LOCOMOTION

The two previous chapters have dealt with the intake or synthesis of high-energy compounds and the manner in which these may be treated to release their energy in a form utilisable by the animal or plant. It has been pointed out that this energy is required for the performance of work. In this chapter it is proposed to give some account of the manner in which mechanical work is performed by living things where locomotion is involved.

Some kind of movement is usually readily discernible in most organisms. It may vary between activity within a cell, activity of an organ, and activity of the whole organism. For example, movement may be restricted to some or all of the protoplasm of a cell. The cytoplasm may stream, or some of its inclusions such as chloroplasts or mitochondria may have their positions altered. Chromosomes may move along a spindle. In other cases, whole organs such as an eye or a leg may undergo movement, whilst in others the whole body may be propelled from place to place. It is this change in position of the whole body which is termed locomotion.

Locomotion is much more characteristic of animals than of plants, where it is confined to a few of the lower groups. The reason for this is not difficult to find. It is bound up very closely with the differing modes of nutrition. The plant is best able to perform its synthesising activities when it is in continuous contact with both its light energy source and the solution in the soil which forms its source of inorganic nutrients. A sedentary existence is therefore a necessity for all plants except aquatics, and even here the powers of locomotion are only an advantage when light and nutrient sources are likely to fluctuate rapidly. Animals, on the other hand, have to seek their elaborated nutrient requirement over wide fields in the great majority of cases. Thus locomotion is as much essential to the animal as the opposite is to the plant. There are, of course, other advantages gained by an organism which is freely motile. The seeking of mates, the avoidance of enemies and of over-crowding are such advantages. There is one period in the life history of all organisms exhibiting sexual reproduction (except the most advanced plants) when free locomotion of a part is essential to the continuance of the species. This is the period during which movement of at least one gamete is essential in order to effect fertilisation.

The advantages accruing to the animal which possesses powers of locomotion can be considered responsible for the evolution of more complex and efficient organs for movement, and with these, greater complexity and efficiency of other systems associated with

them, such as the nervous and vascular systems. It is also possible
to regard the requirement for rapid movement as being the under-
lying cause of the increase in size of multicellular animals, since the
larger an animal is, within limits, the greater its powers of rapid
progression.

[Vines and Rees, *Plant and Animal Biology*, Vol. 11, 4th ed. (Pitman
1972) pp. 458–9)]

(a) *Linear/sequential list notes*

1 *Movement*: found in most organisms

May be:
(A) *Within cell*:
cytoplasm streaming (chloroplasts/mitochondria)
chromosome (along spindle)

(B) *Of whole organ*:
eye/leg

(C) *Of whole organism* = LOCOMOTION
Locomotion ← feeding habits
∴

(1) Few plants:
Light, water, minerals available without locomotion (except
aquatics):
advantage to be sedentary

(2) All animals:
  (i)   Find food (wide area)
  (ii) Find mates
  (iii) Avoid enemies
  (iv) Avoid crowding
  (v) Essential in union of gametes (*plants as well*)
  (vi) Other advantages:
    – evolve better organs of locomotion →
    – better nervous/vascular systems
  (vii) Increased size → increased speed

(b)   *Patterned notes*

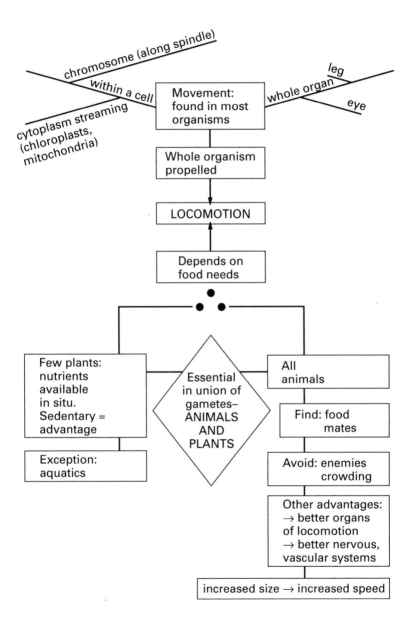

7. Essay Writing

'Reading maketh a full man . . . and writing an exact man.'
[Francis Bacon]

(1) Why Write Essays?

The first point to establish is that the requirement to write essays is not meant to be an institutional burden forced on you by sadistic academics. Essay writing is important for the following reasons:

(a) It forces you to re-work your notes, to take possession of and understand your material thoroughly, to organise your thinking.

(b) It helps you to practise the crucial skill of expressing your ideas on paper with clarity and persuasiveness. This is not just important in terms of academic success, but is central to your development as a thinking person.

(c) It represents a measurement of your progress, enabling both you and those who teach you to identify strengths and weaknesses.

(d) It provides vital material for future examination revision.

(e) It gives you important practice in a skill which is of fundamental importance in the examination situation . . . and in many other aspects of your life.

(f) It may in some circumstances represent part of the coursework which contributes to your final grade.

To be able to express your views and define your conclusions in the context of your own considered writing is to take the final step which *completes the process of study.*

If you remain unconvinced of the vital importance of developing your skill in writing essays, a glance at the examiners' reports published annually by the major examining boards should serve to motivate you. Poor grades and a depressing level of under-achievement are often attributed in these reports to inadequate essay technique, in particular:

● Failing to comprehend precisely the requirements of the question and to structure the answer accordingly.

● Taking insufficient account of such key-words as 'criticise', 'discuss', 'illustrate' and so on.

● Ignoring vital aspects of the question and wandering into irrelevance.

● Recounting or narrating material in a continuous flow without analysing or commenting upon it.

● Failing to pursue a coherent line of thought and to organise material logically.

Faults such as these are found in examination essays at most levels in the majority of subjects.

We are dealing here with the very stuff of academic progress and ultimate success.

(2) The First Steps

(a) Many problems in essay writing arise from a confused view of precisely what the question is asking for. Thus, your first concern must be to ask yourself *precisely* what the question means. Check the meaning of specialist words and phrases or of difficult vocabulary. Examine closely the key words in the topic which will indicate the kind of treatment and general approach required. Is it a request for your personal opinion or does it test your knowledge of other people's ideas? Is it a general over-view or a detailed scrutiny of a particular section? Are you expected to refer to any specific sources of information or technical data? Above all, consider – and *learn* – the precise meanings of the following words or phrases which feature commonly in essay topics. It is of vital importance to understand and to *act upon your understanding* of the differences between these various instructions; there is all the difference in the world between 'Describe Mussolini's rise to power' and 'Explain Mussolini's rise to power'.

Important Words in Essay Questions

Account for   Explain the *reasons* for, giving an indication of all relevant circumstances. Very different from 'Give an account of', which asks only for a detailed description.

Analyse   Study in depth, identifying and describing in detail the main characteristics.

Assess   Examine closely, with a view to measuring or 'weighing up' a particular situation. Consider in a balanced way: strengths and weaknesses, points for and against. In conclusion, state your judgement clearly.

Comment   State clearly and in a moderate fashion your opinions on the material in question. Support your views with references to suitable evidence or with explanation as appropriate.

Compare   Look for qualities or characteristics that resemble each other. Emphasise similarities but be aware also of points of difference.

Contrast   Stress the dissimilarities and differences between the items in question, but do not ignore points of similarity.

Criticise   Express your balanced judgement about the merit or truth of the material in question. Give the results of your scrutiny, establishing both strengths and weaknesses. Be specific.

Define   Give concise, clear and authoritative meanings. Do not give too many details, but be sure to state the limits of the definition. Show how the thing you are defining differs from things in other categories.

Describe   Recount, characterise, sketch or relate in sequence or story form.

Discuss   Examine and analyse carefully, giving reasons pro and con, advantages and disadvantages. Be complete, and give details. You must consider all sides of the issue and reach a balanced conclusion.

Enumerate   State in list or outline form, giving points concisely one by one.

Evaluate   Carefully appraise the matter in hand, citing both advantages and limitations. Emphasise the views of authorities as well as your personal estimation.

Explain   Clarify, interpret and spell out the material you present. Give reasons for important features or developments, and try to analyse causes.

How Far . . .   Similar to questions based on the 'To what extent . . .' approach. Here you are expected to make your case or present your material in the usual way, while remaining aware of the possible need to introduce contradictory or counter-balancing evidence. You are unlikely to be making a 'one hundred per cent' case with this sort of question; careful assessment and weighting are called for.

Illustrate Use specific examples, allusions, figures or diagrams to explain, demonstrate or clarify a problem, situation or view.

Interpret   Translate, give examples of, express in simple terms

	or comment on a subject, usually giving your judgement about it.
Justify	Prove, make out a case or give reasons for decisions or conclusions, taking pains to be convincing.
List	As in 'enumerate', write an itemised series of concise statements.
Outline	Provide a framework description under main points and subordinate points, omitting minor details and stressing the arrangement or classification of the material.
Prove	Establish that something is true by citing factual evidence or giving clear logical reasons.
Relate	Show how things are related to or connected with each other, or how one causes another, correlates with another, or is like another.
Review	Examine a subject critically, analysing and commenting on the important points and stages of development.
State	Present the main points in brief, clear sequence.
Summarise	Give the main points or facts in condensed form, omitting details and illustrations.
Trace	Describe in narrative form progress, development or sequence of events from some point of origin.

Sometimes the topic will contain a combination of two or more of the above instructions, for example 'Describe and explain', which calls for a balance of a) factual account and b) analysis of reasons. In this sort of question it is vital to ensure that you attend to *all* aspects of the instruction. If you do not, you will be marked out of only half or perhaps one third of the total.

Thus, your first task must be to understand precisely what the title is requiring you to do.

(b) Before proceeding further, give some thought to the following list of points, all of which are of great importance when you are faced with the task of writing an essay:

(i)   Good preparation.
(ii)   Sound organisation and planning.
(iii)   Importance of introduction and conclusion.
(iv)   Development of ideas and line of argument.
(v)   Control of material and relevance.
(vi)   Use of quotations and evidence to support each point.
(vii)   Creation of a suitable prose-style: formal, moderate, avoiding extreme expressions, slang and colloquialisms.

(c) The first point, good preparation, is of primary significance. When you have clearly understood what the question asks you to do, you will almost certainly need to do some research to provide you with appropriate material for your essay. It is a great mistake to start wading through notes and books in the hope of a sudden dawning of inspiration. *You need to be analytical and selective in seeking out your material. Give yourself pointers to follow.*
Go back to the topic and jot down as many 'sub-questions' as possible which stem from the topic and to which your essay should in the end provide the answer.

For example:

Topic: *Analyse the case for electoral reform in Great Britain*
You might come up with the following sub-questions:

(i)   What is our present system of voting?

(ii)   How long have we had this system? What preceded it?

(iii)   How accurately is the will of the electorate reflected in our election results?

(iv)   What recent changes have there been? Why were these introduced?

(v) What are the most common criticisms of our present system?

(vi) What are the advantages of the present system?
(a) Easily understood.
(b) Provides 'strong' governments and avoids coalitions.

(vii) What are the points in favour of proportional representation? Explain the various proposed schemes of proportional representation.

(viii) What are the disadvantages of these alternative systems?

(ix) How would the British public respond to extensive change?

And so on . . .

You will be able to compile a list of sub-questions such as these for *any* essay question, thus giving yourself *a way into the topic*, rather than reflecting upon it in general as a rather daunting labour.

You may already know the answers to your sub-questions and have the material for them at your fingertips. If not, jot down next to each one details of where you expect to be able to find the necessary facts or information – perhaps from certain sections of your notes or from books which you know or which have been recommended to you. You may need to use text-books, reference books, encyclopaedias or press articles. Seek help from teaching and library staff. *Record your sources*, for you will need to acknowledge these in your final essay by adding a bibliography, possibly annotated.

(3) Even now you are not ready to leap into the first sentence of your final essay, for you will soon run out of ideas or lose the thread of what you wish to say. You must think out the structure of your essay in its entirety before writing anything; in other words, you need a plan. There are many advantages in making a plan, including the following:

- It helps you to identify and clarify in your mind the main points and the most suitable order in which to deal with them.

- It helps to ensure that nothing is left out and that there is no idle drifting into repetition.

- It gives a sense of purpose and confidence.

- If you run out of time in an examination, a clear plan included at the end of your paper will gain you some marks.

The first step is to write down in just a few sentences your own 'mini-answer' to the question, perhaps in just six or eight lines. This will clear your mind, give you a sense of purpose and direction and enable you to decide on the general trend of your plan.
Having done this, select from your research material what is most relevant to your purpose. Remember that you will need evidence and facts to support all of your assertions, but do not pack in too much supporting material, and do avoid the temptation to work everything in simply because you have made notes and are determined to use them! The art often lies as much in what you leave out as in what you include.

(a) *Making an Outline Plan*

A common essay length is 1200–1500 words, which amounts perhaps to approximately four sides of A4. This will give you scope for between eight and twelve main paragraphs.
Understand at the outset that the unit of the paragraph is of central importance to your developing skills as an essayist. Paragraph divisions are not arbitrary. Each paragraph should deal with a particular point or theme of fundamental significance to the topic. Perhaps the 'topic sentence' – that is the 'lead sentence' which establishes the subject of the paragraph – will be the first of the paragraph, or you may choose to leave it to the end, leading up to it as a kind of climax. In any event, get into the habit of thinking of each paragraph as a building block in the overall plan, and identify your topic sentences as you proceed.

(b) *Design of Essay Plans*

There are several standard approaches to essay design, some of which are listed below:

(i) **Chronological** (according to order in time). With this approach, you order the material and your analysis in the order in which events took place. This is obviously common in history essays, but often also applies to literature essays (sequence of plot development, order of poems and so on) and to many sociological topics.

(ii) **The comparative/thematic approach.** Used when comparing and contrasting two things, for example the hinterland of the ports of Rotterdam and London; this kind of topic should be dealt with point by point/theme by theme, rather than by devoting a large independent section to each side of the question, and thus running the danger of ending up with two 'mini-essays' tacked together.

(iii) **According to points in a discussion.** When examining a particular case in a 'discuss' essay, one block of paragraphs could contain all of the points 'for' with another block embodying all of the points 'against'. Some people prefer the alternating approach of 'point for – point against'. Try to keep the two sides fairly equal. Indicate in the conclusion your view of which side of the argument is the stronger. In other words, beware of 'sitting on the fence', though equally you should beware of adopting an 'all black or all white' approach.

(iv) **Developing from simple to complex.** With this approach, you start by sketching in a general overview, before proceeding to a more detailed approach.

No matter what your choice of plan structure, be consistent and coherent once the choice is made. Logical order is important.

With a carefully thought-out plan (such as the specimen below, which relates to the essay question examined earlier), together with selected notes from your preliminary research, you should be in a position to make a confident start to your essay.

(c) *Specimen Plan*

Analyse the case for electoral reform in Great Britain

   (i)   Introduction

- General Election results regularly reveal the 'unfairness' of present system, especially to third parties.

- We have multi-party system, but election arrangements favour two-party ∴ fail to reflect accurately the opinions of the electorate.

   (ii)   Present system

- How it operates: 'first past the post', winner takes all, single member constituencies.

   (iii)   Advantages of present system

- Simple to operate and understand.

- Quick, normally clear-cut results: said to produce 'strong' government.

- Small constituency: good links with one MP.

   (iv)   Criticisms of present system

- Does not allocate seats in proportion to totals of votes cast: Liberal Democrats suffer from this (get figures).

- Many people's votes 'wasted': majority of 20 000 worth no more than majority of one.

- Parties can form government without gaining majority of total votes (Labour in February 1974).

- A party can get fewer votes than another party but still form the government (Tories, 1951: Labour, February 1974).

- System reinforces 'adversarial' politics: clash of two major parties.

- Does not always produce clear majority (1910, 1923, 1929, February 1974).

(v)   Suggested reforms

- Party list (definition).

- Alternative vote (definition).

- Second ballot (definition).

- Single transferable vote in multi-member constituencies (definition).

(vi)   Advantages of proportional representation

- Result reflects balance of electorate's wishes.

- Greater voice for minority parties.

(vii)   Disadvantages of proportional representation

- Complex to operate and difficult to understand.

- Coalition governments? Critics claim proportional representation provides weak, 'patched together' governments (Italy), yet some work well – Holland, Germany.

- Weakens link of MP with constituents.

(viii) Conclusion

- Strong theoretical case for reform.

- But major parties seeing their support diminish are unlikely to accept proportional representation and threaten their chances of forming a future 'strong' government.

● Electorate does not like radical change: not, as yet, calling in large numbers for reform ∴ unlikely in near future.

(4) Some experts claim that essays should be fully written out twice: once as a first draft, to be followed by a final version. Others, perhaps more realistically, claim that if your preliminary research and outline plan are good enough, then it is desirable to write out the essay only once; they advance the further claim that this is a more realistic preparation for the rigours of essay writing in examination conditions. In any event, it is almost certainly best to write your essay (first or second draft) *at one sitting* of perhaps one and a half to two hours. Do not 'peck at it', doing perhaps fifteen minutes one day, half an hour the next and so on. This is certain to lead to poor continuity and is a dreadful preparation for the examination situation. Essays are best done at home in an atmosphere of quiet and uninterrupted concentration, rather than in a common-room.

(5) Writing Your Essay

Do follow your plan, ensuring that you are ordering your material in a logical way and making your paragraph divisions significant; these act as crucial 'sign-posts' to your reader as he works his way through.

(a) *Introductory Paragraph*

This is of fundamental importance. It should effectively introduce the topic and may vary in length. Its aim is to indicate what will follow, what your approach will be and what you intend to achieve. Often it may include an interpretation of the topic and a brief survey of the key points involved in the topic, helping your reader to see what you believe to be the chief issues. *Avoid reaching your conclusion in the introduction.* Your introduction should not be a precis of your whole answer. It should, however, make specific reference to the actual title, even the actual wording of the title.

(b) *Main Body*

Try to aim for a tone of balance and moderation; consider the facts, express your views, but do not be aggressively dogmatic. Keep to the subject and ensure that everything you write is *relevant*, in other words that it contributes to answering the question. Following your plan, you must develop through clearly defined paragraphs, each with an identifiable topic and theme. One paragraph should lead smoothly and logically to the next. Support each main opinion or statement with evidence, examples, illustrations, quotations. *Remember to acknowledge your sources and to avoid plagiarism*, which is the unacknowledged copying of material from another person's book or article. When quoting from a work, enter a reference number after the quotation, thus enabling your reader to check the source in the references section at the end of your essay.

Do avoid above all the recurring error of simple narration (particularly common in history, literature and other 'narrative' essays); *your comment and analysis are needed*.

(c) *Comment and Analysis*

A useful rule of thumb to bear in mind – whatever the subject on which you are writing – is:

(i)   Present the evidence or primary material.
(ii) Make your comments.
(iii) Draw your conclusion.

The order may often be altered – (i) and (ii), for instance, are frequently reversed – but this is more a matter of style than substance. The essential point is to remember and implement at all stages of your essay this basic three-point plan.

There follows an example of how the plan would work in a literature essay. The essayist is discussing the characterisation of Widmerpool, an important figure in the opening novel of Anthony Powell's series *A Dance to the Music of Time*:

> The early description of Widmerpool is particularly illuminating:

Evidence/ Primary Material	'His status was not high. He had no colours, and although far from being a dunce, there was nothing notable about his work.' His sporting endeavour is laboured as when he is described on the water: ' . . . rowing "courses" on the river, breathing heavily, the sweat clouding his thick lenses, while he dragged his rigger through the water.' His achievements are scant: 'So far as I know he never reached even the semi-finals of the events for which he used to enter. Most of the time he was alone, and even when he walked with other boys, he seemed in some ways separate from them.' [Anthony Powell, *A Question of Upbringing* (Fontana, 1984) p. 8]
Comments	The general impression here is of a mediocrity, somebody who puts in a great deal of uninspired effort, but never achieves anything out of the ordinary. Widmerpool's thick lenses seem to imply a rather dull and bookish individual. His isolation is clearly established.
Conclusion	It seems reasonable to assume that one is making acquaintance with a rather solitary and alienated character, perhaps even an object of derision.

Check throughout the writing of your essay that you are following the three-point plan: evidence/comment/conclusion.

(d) *Quotations*

There are several points to be made about the use of quotations:

(i)   There is no particular virtue in using very lengthy quotations in your essays; this tends to distract attention from the thread of your argument and to give the impression that you are uncertain or tentative about your own contribution. Protracted quotations in examination essays waste time and imply that you are trying to 'work in' a specially revised piece. Be selective; prune and trim the material until it suits your purposes.

(ii) If you wish to show that you are referring to a whole speech, quote the opening section and follow with a row of dots:
Shortly after quitting the performance of the travelling players, Claudius is seen to be deeply disturbed:
'O, my offence is rank, it smells to heaven . . .'

(iii) Use rows of dots to take the place of any unnecessary sections in your quotations, whether a small number of words or several whole lines.

(iv) You can use a row of dots to separate two or more consecutive quotations:

Hamlet often criticises himself fiercely, as in the soliloquy following the player's recital:
'O what a rogue and peasant slave am I . . .'
'. . . it cannot be
But I am pigeon-livered . . .'
'Why, what an ass am I . . .'

(v) You can use a quotation to round off or conclude the meaning of one of your own sentences, using a dash to lead the eye into the quotation: A simple definition of our invisible exports would be that they represent – ' . . . those services which are sold by residents of the UK to other nationals.' [J. F. Nicholson, *Modern British Economics* (Allen & Unwin, 1973) p. 132]

(vi) You can develop your own sentence into a quotation and complete it afterwards, using dashes to lead into and out of the quotation:

In view of the deteriorating economic situation in France –
' . . . the assignat had been falling rapidly and by July 1793 had lost 77 per cent of its face value . . .'

– the populace of Paris was in considerable ferment, and posed a threat to the Committee of Public Safety.
[Alfred Cobban, *A History of Modern France*, Vol. 1 (Penguin, 1962) p. 221]

(vii) Short quotations of a word or phrase, suitably indicated, may be incorporated into your own sentence:
Italian rococo furniture was often 'very roughly made' in terms of actual quality, though possessing in appearance a 'distinctly theatrical air' and a certain 'carnival spirit'.
[Edward Lucie-Smith, *Furniture: A Concise History* (Thames & Hudson, 1979) p. 102]

Note

● If quoting from a verse play or from a poem, your quotation must retain the original line structure.

● Avoid the common mistake of using a quotation without explaining the context. Many students are inclined to write something like:

> Lady Macbeth is a fiercely ruthless woman:
> 'But screw your courage to the sticking place,
> And we'll not fail . . .'

This is, of course, insufficient, and tends to give a rather casual, 'take it or leave it' impression. It needs to be amplified along the following lines:

> Lady Macbeth is a fiercely ruthless woman, as is seen when she scornfully rejects her husband's fear of failing in the attempt to murder Duncan:
> 'But screw your courage . . .

Crisp and appropriate use of quotation in your essay will give a distinct air of competence, an impression that you are on top of your material and well able to turn it to your advantage.

(e) *Conclusion*

This should sum up the main points in the essay and emphasise your final considered view. Make sure that you answer in your conclusion any questions posed by the topic. Some people suggest drafting your conclusion first, so that you have a sense of purpose and direction. *Avoid simply repeating the points made in your introduction.* It is important also to avoid expressing views in your concluding paragraph that are at odds with those expressed earlier.

At the end of your essay, you must give details of the publications from which you have drawn. This is done in two sections:

(i)   References
       List here, in order, the sources of the quotations which you have used and numbered in the text of your essay. For example:
       1. John Peck, *How to Study a Novel* (Macmillan, 1983) p. 47.

(ii)   Bibliography
       List here all of the books which you have used or consulted, whether or not you have quoted from them. Entries should be in alphabetical order of the authors' surnames. For example:
       Cunliffe, Marcus, *The Literature of the United States* 3rd ed. (Penguin, 1967)
       Williams, Raymond, *Keywords* (Fontana, 1976).

(f) *Prose Style*

Aim for formal, unemotional language. Slang must be avoided at all costs. Be concise; do not allow your sentences to wander into enormous length. If a single sentence will do, do not expand into a whole paragraph. Clarity of expression depends on clarity of thought; if you have prepared your plan properly, you will have a clear sense of what you are seeking to achieve and should be able to avoid vagueness.

(i)   Aim for a combination of short and long sentences.

(ii)   Avoid florid, over-ornate language, full of over-blown adjectives and pompous phrasing.

(iii) Avoid expressions of frenzied enthusiasm. Gushing prose – ' . . . this is a truly wise and wonderful book . . .' – will impress nobody.

(iv)   Try to avoid the habit of beginning sentences with the same word or phrase.

(v)   Avoid the use of personal pronouns – I, you, us.

(vi)   Never use side-headings or numbered points in an essay.

(vii) Avoid the constant use of brackets; these are seldom needed.

(viii) Never abbreviate words – Parl. for Parliament, Jan. for January and so on.

(ix)   Never split words between the end of one line and the beginning of another.

(x)   Avoid irritating colloquialisms such as 'got', 'a lot of', 'nice', 'around this time'.

(xi)   Numbers from one to one hundred should be written in full; numbers above one hundred may be shown as numerals. Numerals are acceptable for days of the month and years, as well as for statistics and page and chapter references.

(g) *Presentation*

It is bad manners – and from a student's point of view, bad tactics – to submit an essay in scrawled or indecipherable handwriting. If you have a problem in this connection, try to type your work. Even better, if you have your own PC at home, is to word-process it. This will give you the obvious advantages of easy addition/deletion/

correction/shifting of text, without the traditional angst of ripping up sheet after sheet of paper. You are also likely to find that you have access to the program's built-in thesaurus and spell-check, though you should not place too much trust in the latter; perfectly correct spellings of unusual words and names are sometimes rejected by the spell-check facility in favour of exotically incorrect alternatives! A further advantage of word-processing your work is that you are able to call up a variety of print styles and fonts. Whether you use a typewriter or word-processor, the quality of finish is likely to lend an air of professionalism to what you have produced. However, do not forget to check – as suggested in Chapter 2 – if there are any restrictions on the number of word-processed assignments that may be submitted.

Finally, do try to regard the return of a marked essay as an opportunity to learn, to improve your style and general essay approach. Look at the essays written by other members of your group, to see how they have addressed the question. Discuss your answers, and differing approaches, with each other.

Remember that you are practising a 'life skill' as well as a study technique.

Above all, be determined:

'A man may write at any time, if he will set himself doggedly to it.' [Dr Samuel Johnson]

8. Projects

Although the traditional essay remains the usual form of continuous writing on most courses, many students are faced with the requirement to produce an extended piece of work, most often known as a project, though sometimes referred to as a long essay or dissertation (see Glossary).

(1) Some of the chief characteristics of such a task are as follows:

(a) You will have a considerable time to complete the work; this sounds like an advantage, but can cause problems if inertia sets in or if you fail to develop a momentum.

(b) Most likely you will not be given a 'set' topic. There will probably be scope for your own identifying of an area that interests you, to be followed by discussion with your teacher or tutor so as to finalise the topic. Because of this, you will be faced with the need to work independently of others, for you are not likely to be covering the same ground as your fellow students.

(c) You will need to carry out a considerable amount of research, gathering from a variety of sources information, material and statistics relevant to your topic. Clear note-making is vital here.

(d) Your final version will need to be written up in accordance with certain formal rules of presentation.

It is clear that preparing a project will call upon all of the study skills outlined hitherto. The challenge and value of such a task, however, are beyond doubt and not simply a matter of the quality of the end product. Many experts would say that the independence of action and judgement, the marshalling of resources and sheer organisation involved in preparing an extended project are just as important – perhaps more important – than the finished article itself.

(2) Important Points

(a) You must establish a *broad outline timetable* for yourself. Consider your final deadline, then work backwards, establishing a series of interim deadlines. Once your topic is finalised, you will need to fix these deadlines for each of the following stages:

(i)   End of research and gathering of material.
(ii) Completion of first rough draft and submission for comment.
(iii) Completion of revision and amendments.
(iv) To be followed, of course, by the final presentation. Your final writing up of the project must not overlap with time needed for examination revision. Make sure that your outline timetable takes account of this. Try to finish early.

(b) Having established an outline timetable, you must ensure that your weekly schedule has one or more allocations of time to be spent on the project. It is essential that you sustain *continuity of involvement* with the work, particularly when you have several months in which to complete. Do not let your interest or attention lapse. Re-read regularly what you have already completed and jot down ideas for further development as they come to you. Remain actively engaged.

(3) Selecting a Topic

In deciding on a topic for your project, the following points are important:

(a) While projects may sometimes argue a case or promote a particular opinion, they are more often likely to be reviews of situations or descriptive accounts, drawing together material from different sources to present a coherent and well supported overview.

(b) There are several approaches to a topic:

(i) The macro – the general, wide-ranging picture of an extensive subject. A student of comparative religion wishing to adopt this approach might select a topic such as 'The World of Islam'.

(ii) The micro – a far more detailed scrutiny of a narrow and clearly focused area. An example from media studies could be a topic such as 'Developments in Cable Television'.

(iii) The historical – this has the apparent advantage of dealing with something complete, over and done with and therefore capable of rational and balanced judgement. A student of military history might find this kind of appeal in a topic dealing with 'The Role of Tanks in the First World War'.

(iv) The current – perhaps more challenging, though obviously more uncertain and open to a variety of interpretations. An example from the social sciences: 'Trends in Juvenile Crime'.

(c) You must ensure that you have a genuine interest in your topic and that it is not an unrealistic aim. Too broad an area will lead inevitably to a sketchy and superficial approach, as will soon be realised by a student opting for a topic of intimidating breadth, such as 'World Energy: Patterns of Supply and Consumption'. On the other hand, too narrow a field could mean undue specialist detail or problems in finding material, as the same student would be likely to find on readjusting his aim to 'Waste Heat from Power Stations'. As always, a balance must be sought. A topic such as 'Oil from the North Sea' seems to offer an appropriate blend of such factors as clearly defined geographical area, scope for history of development, technical data, human interest and so on.

(d) If you are having difficulty in finding a topic, take any area of study or essay question that has interested you in the recent past and compile a list of 'sub-questions' as suggested in the chapter on essay writing; this may well throw up an interesting starting point. For instance, a student of commerce who had enjoyed a lecture on the high street banks might compile a list including:

What was the early development of the banking system?

What is the history of the cheque?

How does 'clearing' take place?

How does the use of banking facilities vary according to social class?

What are the most and least used facilities offered by banks?

What is the personnel structure and normal work-load of a typical local bank?

What is the history so far and the possible future development of automated banking – cash dispensers and so on?

Given the use of credit and bank cards, are we approaching a 'cash-less' society?

How do banks acquire and record the foreign currency used in exchange?

What are the foreign involvements of the major banks?

What are the typical security arrangements of a bank for transfer of cash, computer transactions and so on?

How are safe deposit boxes operated?

How are staff trained?

Such a list will contain the seeds of several possible project topics. The secret of finding a topic at this stage, then, is to take an area that interests you and write down as many 'offshoot questions' as possible.

(e) You must discuss your proposed topic fully with your teacher or tutor in order to gain an expert opinion on its viability.

(4) You must begin with a plan, just as you would with an essay; do not simply wander into the early stages in the vague hope that the ideas will flow. Be clear about what you hope to achieve in each section. Imagine that our commerce student had settled on 'An outline history of banking' as a topic. A possible plan, following a basically chronological approach, might be as follows:

(a) Primitive forms of barter: problems of comparability, portability, flexibility.

(b) Development of currency: shells and beads, gold and silver, coinage.

(c) Pre-requisites of a system of coinage: scarcity, acceptability, divisibility.

(d) How coin is handled by banks at present.

(e) The history of bank notes.

(f) The development of cheques.

(g) Growth of the lending and investment function.

(h) Mergers and take-overs leading to the system of clearing banks: definition.

(i) Systems of credit.

(j) The role of the Bank of England.

As with an essay, the main approaches are chronological (as above), comparative/thematic, general to detailed. See Chapter 7 for fuller details.

(5) Before beginning to collect material, list *all* of the sources that you intend to use, giving, if appropriate, a brief description of what you hope to gain from each. This will give you a sense of purpose and direction. Sources could include any or all of the following:

(a) *Libraries:* Search through the catalogue and list any titles likely to be of use. Go through the shelves of the reference section and add to your list the details of any books that may be relevant. Not only books, but periodicals, technical papers, reports and so on. Scan each (Chapter 4) for usefulness. In certain subject areas – for instance the social sciences – you may be able to gain access to computerised banks of data/statistical information. The advantage of this is that, instead of working laboriously with printed tables of figures in published format, you are able to sit at the keyboard and ask direct questions tailored to your area of research. A further possibility offered by computerisation in this area is the scope for working with statistical 'models'. For example, you might have a model of a hypothetical country's economy which would allow you to make policy decisions, enter information and examine likely outcomes. Be sure to ask the library assistants for any guidance that you may need; as long as you do not expect them to do the work for you, they will be pleased to help.

(b) *Personal contact:* If writing to an individual or institution for information or material, make your request both clear and polite. Enclose a stamped, self-addressed envelope.

If telephoning, do ask if it is a convenient time and if not, be prepared to call back. Have your questions ready and keep pencil and paper at your side.

If you are able to fix a personal interview, be prompt, polite and precise. Once again, you must have your questions ready and not waste the other person's time. Tape-recording *must* have the approval of the other party.

(c) *On-site visits*:   Do not simply show up at an office, factory or other venue. Write or telephone so as to secure permission in advance. You should not take photographs or interview members of the work-force unless you are clearly permitted to do so.

(d) *Surveys*:   If you have constructed a questionnaire, make sure it has the approval of your teacher/tutor. The questions should be balanced, realistic and not unduly intrusive. Have a 'dry-run' with a small number of family and friends before launching the main exercise; such a precaution may well indicate desirable alterations in format. Do not jump to wild conclusions as a result of your findings.

Note

Whenever you make a personal approach to an individual or organisation for help, you will find it useful to have a letter of accreditation from your place of study. *Always* express your thanks for help received.

(6) Recording your Material

From all of the above sources you will gather a mass of material that must be set down in usable and efficient note form. The basic techniques are as outlined in Chapter 6. Because of the sheer volume of the material collected for a substantial project, however, it is probably advisable to adopt a special strategy as follows:

(a) Establish a separate folder in which to construct a directory of your sources:

(i) Books and periodicals: set down the name of the author, the title of the book or article, the publisher, the edition and date of publication.

(ii) Personal contacts: set down the name of the person contacted, his official position, the institution represented, the date of the contact.

(iii) Personal observation: set down the time, date and place of your visit, together with an indication of the main areas of interest.

(b) The notes themselves are best kept – for purposes of availability, flexibility and selective pruning – on small file cards in an alphabetically indexed box file. Restrict yourself to one main noted item or a closely linked sequence of items per card. *Do not write on both sides of a card.* The top of each card should show:

The subject of the note
The source

For example:

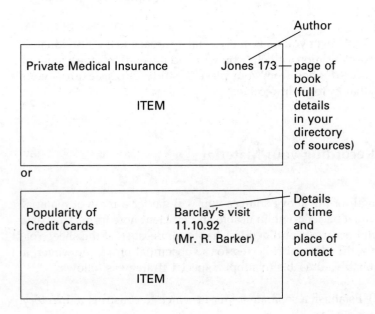

Author

| Private Medical Insurance | Jones 173 | page of book (full details in your directory of sources) |

ITEM

or

| Popularity of Credit Cards | Barclay's visit 11.10.92 (Mr. R. Barker) | Details of time and place of contact |

ITEM

If you have your own PC, you will find it very useful for storing and manipulating certain types of information. For example, you can create your own data base to record details which have a common and recurring format, whilst a spreadsheet will enable you to enter and work flexibly with numerical information. Once your information is entered in data base or spreadsheet, you will be able to call it up in a variety of formats and graphical displays.

(7) Writing Up

When you have finished gathering your note-form material, sit down with your outline plan and file cards. Fix the plan carefully in your mind, then read through your note-cards. Eliminate any that are not relevant to your purpose; avoid the temptation to include material simply because you have spent time on it. Now is the time to move away from the alphabetical ordering of the remaining cards; stack them in sections relating to the main stages of your plan and clip or tie each section of cards together.

You are now in a position to begin writing up. Follow the general rules set forth in the chapter on essay writing (Chapter 7). A point worth stressing is that a project even more than an essay tempts some students to copy out verbatim long extracts from printed sources. Do avoid this. By all means quote from books or articles, but make it clear that you are doing so by using numbered references and remember that the continuous seam running through the whole project must be *your* views and *your* observations in *your* words.

List your references (see Chapter 7) at the end of the project, and remember that such references may be used not only to record sources of quotations, but also to refer the reader to related points in other parts of your project. For example:

1.   The issue of occupation-related illness is explored more fully in Chapter 2, page 14.

This technique of 'cross-referencing' is a great help to your reader, and indicates a professional and analytical approach on your part.

By all means illustrate your project with photographs, drawings, graphs, tables, charts and so on. Make sure, however, that such material is relevant to the part of the text in which it is presented, and that you are not using it simply as decoration. Remember that an illustration *must* be well presented, or it will have a negative effect. Chapter 9 gives useful advice on the presentation and layout of diagrams, graphs and tables.

Do not expect your first written version to suffice. Submit it – either in whole or section by section – for comment and criticism, and be prepared to revise in the light of suggestions received.

(8) Final Presentation

It is perfectly acceptable to present your project in handwritten form – as long as it is very neat. Typed presentation is preferable and word-processed better still. The latter has all of the advantages enumerated in Chapter 7; if you are also able to use a desk-top publishing program, you will have at your disposal such facilities as headlining, column format and the ability to present illustrations/graphs/maps and so on inside page frames. Whatever your choice of presentation, use only one side of the paper and include in the following order:

(a) A title page, showing the name of your place of education, the title of the project, your own name and the year of writing.

(b) (Optional). An acknowledgement of particular help received.

(c) A contents page giving *full* chapter titles and page numbers.

(d) (If appropriate). A list of maps, diagrams and illustrations, with page numbers.

(e) TEXT OF PROJECT.

(f) (Optional). An appendix or appendixes in which you may present material relevant to your subject, but too substantial to include in the main text.

(g) (If appropriate). A list of people interviewed, their positions, organisations and so on.

(h) A list of numbered references in the order in which they appear in the text.

(i) A full bibliography set out as illustrated in Chapter 7.

9. Other Formats

(1) Diagrams

There is scope for diagrams in most subject areas, but in the sciences – physics, chemistry, biology, geography, geology and so on – they are of central importance. Diagrams of apparatus, equipment and experimental structures are commonplace, while the individual sciences often have specific diagram requirements:

Physics: electrical circuits
                                       optical diagrams

Chemistry: crystal structure
                                       comparative tables (such as
                                       the 'Periodic Table')

Biology: cell and tissue diagrams
                                       'chain diagrams' (such as
                                       food chains)

Geography/Geology: mineral structures
                                       maps

(a) *The Value of Diagrams*

   (i)   For the 'producer' they are an aid in thinking through a situation or problem logically and correctly.

  (ii)   For the 'consumer' they convey ideas, principles and situations more clearly, briefly and efficiently than words.

(iii) They demonstrate the relative size of items, their shape and the spatial relationships between them.

(iv) Accurate diagrams can often compensate for mistakes in written work.

(b) *Important Diagram Skills*

(i) The ability to understand and interpret diagrams; in other words, to see the basic meaning as quickly as possible and to judge if the diagram is likely to have implications in other related situations.

(ii) The ability to *use* specific types of diagram in working out and estimating; a good example would be the use of scale diagrams.

(iii) the ability to remember the information embodied in a diagram, and to reproduce the diagram itself from memory, particularly in examinations (see Chapter 11).

(iv) The ability to design and draw your own diagrams neatly and efficiently in order to set forth or summarise certain facts or information.

(c) *Drawing and Presentation of Diagrams*

Carefully designed and beautifully drawn diagrams represent a fine ideal, to which you should aspire whenever possible. When there is insufficient time, particularly in examinations, most people have to settle for sketch diagrams. Whether you are working at leisure or in haste, the following suggestions should be useful:

(i) Ensure that your diagram appears at the most appropriate point; this is particularly important when it accompanies an extended piece of writing.

(ii) Give your diagram a clear title – and a number, if it is one of several.

(iii) Surround your diagram with a generous margin of 'white space'; it should not be cramped cheek by jowl with written sections. A good diagram deserves at least half a page or so to itself.

(iv) Flasks, beakers and other scientific apparatus are best drawn with the aid of specialist stencils, though these cannot adapt to change of size, and are a little slow to use in examinations. Straight lines must be drawn with a ruler or stencil edge.

(v) A diagram should be completely self-explanatory. For this reason, *labelling* is crucial; every significant part and component of a diagram should be clearly identified.

Labels should not be placed too close to the diagram or they will lessen its visual impact and hinder effective interpretation. Use 'indicator lines' (drawn with a ruler) to keep your labels at a reasonable distance from the diagram itself. Indicator lines may be drawn in pencil and diagram outlines in ink, so as to avoid confusion.

Print your labels neatly; it is often a good idea to underline. If you wish to make a particularly professional job of it, you could use one of the 'dry transfer' lettering kits available from stationers.

(vi) Discreet use of colour – perhaps for shading or emphasising an outline – can often add distinction to a diagram, but do not allow it to become intrusive.

(vii) Pencilled 'construction lines' in a diagram may serve to demonstrate spatial relationships.

(2) Graphs

In mathematics, the sciences and many other disciplines, graphs play a crucial role in demonstrating inter-relationships. Bear in mind the following practical points:

(a) You should use plenty of space; make your axes and scales fill the graph paper.

(b) It is difficult and potentially inaccurate to attempt to focus on and plot a point in two dimensions at once. It may be fairly simple if the point to be plotted coincides with the intersection of two lines on the graph paper, but this is not always the case.

Use a ruler – transparent for preference – or a set square. Position the ruler at right angles to the x-axis (horizontal) and move along until the appropriate value is reached. Now move your pencil up the edge of the ruler until the required y-value (on the vertical axis) is reached. Enter the point with the pencil hard against the edge of the ruler. The marked point should be fine and small

(c) Your first plotting of a point should be in pencil – in case of error. When confirmed, mark it in ink, so as to make it stand out from the line of the graph.

(d) Add visual emphasis to the plotted point by drawing a small, neat circle around it. Chemistry stencils often include suitable circles; if not, use the small letter 'o' from a lettering stencil. Circled points are greatly preferable to crosses or shapeless blobs. If your sheet contains more than one graph, the circles on each may be drawn in contrasting colours.

(e) If each point is to be joined to the next by a straight line, make sure you use a ruler. If you are to link the points with a curve drawn 'free-hand', adopt the following procedure:

   (i) Turn the paper so that your drawing hand is positioned 'inside' the curve.

   (ii) Let the movement of your hand – pivoting at the wrist – trace a broadly accurate route.

   (iii) Without actual contact, run your pencil around the curve to assess the general correctness of your positioning.

(iv) Draw the curve in one sweeping stroke.

The easy and foolproof technique is to buy a 'flexible curve' from your local stationers!

(f) If your graph contains 'constructions' such as tangents and triangles, these must be clearly shown. Different constructions may be drawn in varying colours.

(g) The line or curve of your graph may not always pass through every point, and you should not 'force' it to do so if one point looks to be wildly astray. Instead, you should follow the route dictated by the rest of the points, and check for the experimental error or mistake in reckoning or plotting that may have caused the misplaced point.

(h) Your graph must be clearly labelled. Check the following:

(i) That you have indicated the quantity on each axis: for example, distance and time. Note that 'time' is normally entered on the 'x' or horizontal axis.

(ii) That you have marked the scales on the axes; there must be sufficient gradations for the reader/examiner to check and interpret the information easily.

(iii) That where appropriate, you have given details of units of dimension (for example, seconds or metres) to demonstrate what the numbers refer to.

(iv) That you have entered identifying letters (in block capitals) on the main elements of any constructions in your graph.

(v) That you have a clearly visible title.

(vi) In an examination, that you have appended a question number, so as to link your graph (normally drawn on a separate sheet of paper) with the correct question.

(3) Tables

A table of data is a most useful medium in that it can summarise a very great deal of information.

There are no rigid rules governing lay-out, but the following guide-lines may be useful:

(a) There should be a clear and detailed title, indicating the scope of the information provided.

(b) You should make clear at the top of the table the quantities or multiples in which you are dealing and to which your figures refer.

(c) If your essay or project contains several tables, number them so as to show the chapter in which they belong and their order in the chapter; for example, the identifying number 3.4 indicates that the table in question is the fourth in chapter 3.

(d) As with graphs, a 'time-scale' is most often entered horizontally, with 'categories' listed vertically.
     Make the 'categories' column wide enough to accommodate the lengthiest item.

(e) You must allow sufficient space to separate consecutive vertical columns of figures. Cramping will deny 'visual access' and cause a risk of error in interpretation.

(f) In the vertical entering of 'categories', there must be similarly helpful spacing: to group linked items together, to differentiate one sub-section from another and to divide the information into 'digestible' units.

(g) Sub-section headings should be clearly identified, either by underlining, heavy printing or appropriate use of spacing.

(h) It is now accepted 'tabular convention' to omit the traditional comma in showing thousands. In its place, a space is entered at the appropriate point: thus 5 326. Decimal points should be on the line – not above it.

(i)   Global totals may be entered either in the top or bottom line of your table. However, if you are entering 'intermediate totals' at various stages in your table, these should be clearly and appropriately marked off.

(j)   It is quite in order to use footnotes if you feel that a particular entry in your table needs further explanation in words.

(k)   You should always state your sources.

The publications of the Central Statistical Office represent an object lesson in tabular clarity and in the implementation of the above principles, as will be seen in the example on page 85.

Apart from this full-scale tabular format, there are several other methods of presenting facts and figures in eye-catching style.

Although not strictly speaking a 'table', a *pie chart* is most useful in demonstrating at a glance the importance of different items as a proportion of the whole. The example below shows how the year's sales of a local department store are made up:

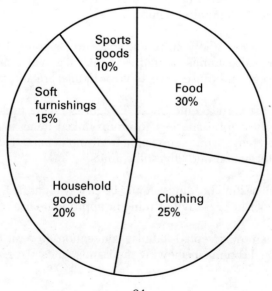

Consumers' expenditure at current market prices: classified by commodity

£ million

	1980	1981	1982	1983	1984	1985	1986	1987	1988	1989	1990
Durable goods:											
Cars, motorcycles and other vehicles	6 510	6 557	7 407	9 112	8 986	9 922	11 498	13 462	17 418	20 274	19 530
Furniture and floor coverings	3 394	3 488	3 615	3 883	3 968	4 193	4 514	5 058	5 951	6 348	6 285
Other durable goods	3 591	3 897	4 417	5 255	5 682	6 136	6 838	7 749	8 565	9 216	9 234
Total	13 495	13 942	15 439	18 250	18 636	20 251	22 850	26 269	31 934	35 838	35 139
Other goods:											
Food (household expenditure)	23 655	24 946	26 490	28 061	29 274	30 657	32 561	34 472	36 593	39 245	41 833
Beer	5 320	5 971	6 450	7 138	7 734	8 416	8 902	9 398	10 039	10 676	11 743
Other alcoholic drink	4 635	5 181	5 553	6 132	6 582	7 235	7 502	8 053	8 715	9 141	9 987
Tobacco	4 821	5 515	5 881	6 209	6 622	7 006	7 471	7 653	7 945	8 196	8 835
Clothing other than footwear	8 113	8 313	8 857	9 824	10 647	12 139	13 663	14 599	15 736	16 533	17 157
Footwear	1 760	1 842	2 068	2 296	2 510	2 772	2 998	3 085	3 192	3 357	3 545
Energy products	11 001	13 422	15 027	16 220	16 959	18 530	18 240	18 527	19 454	20 394	22 383
Other goods	14 601	15 803	17 212	18 764	20 567	22 921	26 113	28 850	32 575	35 285	37 872
Services:											
Rents, rates and water charges	16 153	19 558	22 558	24 057	25 207	27 387	30 003	32 777	36 508	39 398	39 457
Other services[1]	36 054	40 919	45 115	50 077	54 687	60 304	70 972	81 197	96 105	108 426	121 470
Total consumers' expenditure	139 608	155 412	170 650	187 028	199 425	217 618	241 275	264 880	296 796	326 489	349 421

1. Including the adjustments for international travel, etc and final expenditure by private non-profit-making bodies serving persons.
[Adapted from Annual Abstract of Statistics: 1992 (HMSO)]

85

A point to remember before deciding on a pie chart: this approach works best when the number of 'segments' is limited, preferably no more than five or six, and when the figures to be included are fairly simple – otherwise it becomes rather too complex to design and draw.

Instead of a pie chart, the totals may be represented in a *percentage bar chart*, as shown below. This format can accommodate effectively a greater number of component sections than a pie chart. The basic principle is that the entire length of the vertical bar makes up 100 per cent, with its sub-sections drawn proportionately to scale:

Sports goods 10%
Soft furnishings 15%
Household goods 20%
Clothing 25%
Food 30%

It is, of course, possible to remove the words and figures from the boxes themselves, set the whole bar against a numbered vertical axis – in order to establish actual values – and identify the boxes by differential shading or colouring (see page 87 opposite).

This approach may be particularly appropriate when juxtaposing several bars relating to different years, as the varying amounts of shading give a rapid indication of trends. This multiple-bar format is sometimes known as a *histogram*.

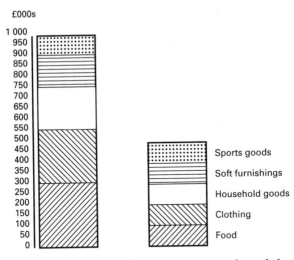

£000s

Because our eyes move with particular ease from left to right, *horizontal bar charts* will often serve to emphasise similarities and differences between component parts:

Food	300 000
Clothing	250 000
Household goods	200 000
Soft furnishings	150 000
Sports goods	100 000

The descending order shown above is a useful device if you wish to establish different sectors in rank order of importance. However, if your intention is to stress inequalities or unevenness, you may prefer to alternate greater with lesser:

Household goods	200 000
Sports goods	100 000
Food	300 000
Soft furnishings	150 000
Clothing	250 000

Once you have entered the relevant information, all of the above formats – tables, pie charts, bar charts etc. – may be readily generated and printed by computers. Another good reason for working with a PC!

(4) Writing Up Experiments

An important aspect of every science course is the practical work, and a particularly significant feature of this is the describing and recording of experiments.

The aim is to present a detailed and accurate description of how an experiment is carried out, what is observed during its course and what conclusions have been reached.

You should standardise on a consistent pattern, such as the following:

Title of experiment	*Date*
Aim	
Apparatus	*Materials*
List here each piece of equipment used.	List here any materials or substances, such as chemicals, which are used in the experiment.

[These lists are unlikely to be of similar length; leave a space of two lines beneath the longer list before starting the diagram.]

Diagram

Follow the guide-lines already laid down. You should draw a clear, cross-sectional diagram of any apparatus used, shown as it is assembled for the experiment. Remember the importance of neat and full labelling.

Method

In this section, you should give a careful and complete account of how the experiment was performed. You must specify how the apparatus was used and the nature of any precautions taken to guard against false readings or inaccurate observations.

Describe the experiment in step-by-step fashion, with each stage numbered in sequence. Your account should be in the past tense. There should be no use of personal names or pronouns. The aim is to achieve an objective tone. Thus:

<u>The flask was heated</u> until the solution boiled
rather than
<u>I heated the flask</u> until the solution boiled.

Results and Observations

Here you must describe carefully and in the correct order both what you have observed and the precise results of any measurements you have taken. A sequence of numerical results should be presented in tabular form.

Conclusion

In this closing section you must explain carefully what you have deduced from your results and what you have learned from the experiment.

Note

The above is a generally standard procedure, but there may be preferred variations from one institution to another. Check to ensure that you are not at odds with guide-lines issued in your own establishment.

10. *Understanding, Memory and Recall*

(1) It is essential to realise that you will not understand your material and commit it to memory simply by attending lessons or lectures and occasionally looking through notes and books.

Understanding depends very much on *working with and manipulating* one's material, rather than simply filing it and remaining distanced from it.

The chapter on notes stressed the importance of amplifying them, re-arranging them, possibly rewriting them. Certainly, you must seek for ways of *using* them as soon as possible. Essays present obvious opportunities for this, but so too do general discussion and such projects as preparing for a short talk to your group. The next chapter will demonstrate how important it is to *work* actively with your material when revising for examinations.

No matter what the context, you must realise that *not until you have used your new knowledge will you really feel that you understand it, that it truly belongs to you.* Seek to connect it with what you already know; look for other examples to illustrate it; consider whether it requires you to alter your previous ideas.

(2) Understanding and memory retention do not remain unchanged as time passes. You may understand an idea or theory perfectly well in the first instance, but there is no guarantee that you will be able to understand or recall it some time later.

Consider the following:

(a) You should never try to memorise something that you do not understand.

(b) You tend to recall more readily material covered at the beginnings and ends of learning sessions.

(c) You tend to commit material more readily to memory if it is learned in short sections.

(d) You tend to recall more readily items which are linked in some way by obvious relationship, repetition, rhyme and so on.

(e) You tend to recall more easily items which are somehow outstanding or unusual.

(f) Learning periods of approximately forty to fifty minutes seem to offer in general the best conditions for understanding and later recall. If you plan to study for two to three hours, give yourself breaks so as to leave you with periods of this length.

(g) The bad news: it has been estimated that unless suitable precautions are taken, 75 per cent of the material covered may be forgotten only twenty-four hours after the learning session.

(h) The good news: *you can avoid this loss* by adopting a structured sequence of reviews, with each review timed to strengthen recall at a number of critical points:

Begin with   (i) The original learning session.

Followed by   (ii) Review *fifteen minutes later*, the review itself lasting for about ten to fifteen minutes. This first review should involve thorough re-reading of the material; if you have been working with notes, they should at this stage be expanded, restructured, perhaps rewritten.

Followed by   (iii) Review *twenty-four hours later*, the review lasting for about five minutes. Test recall by writing down all that can be remembered without looking at the material, then fill in any gaps by checking against the original.

Followed by   (iv) Review *one week later*, the review lasting for about three minutes. Test recall as above.

Followed by   (v) Review *one month later*, the review lasting for about three minutes. Test recall as above.

At the end of this five-stage sequence, the material should be fairly securely fixed in the memory, with only occasional brief reminders needed.

The crucial lesson is LEARN – THEN REVIEW. If you fail to do this vital follow-up work, you are wasting your initial effort . . . pouring water in the sand.

(3) Apart from this fundamental technique of *learning followed by regular review*, there are several 'tricks' or tactics which are often used to help memorise difficult or elusive material:

(a) If faced with the need to memorise a list, take the first item and begin inventing a wild story with it, bringing in the other items in the correct order.

(b) Remember the importance of rhyming; even the lamest of rhymes can fix things permanently in the memory. Consider 'Thirty days hath September . . . '. *Make up your own rhymes*; these are even more likely to stay put.

(c) Mnemonics are artificial 'memory-jogging' devices which can help you to memorise virtually anything. Many people make up mnemonics to help them remember telephone numbers, addresses and so on. Approaches are limitless, but may include techniques such as the following:

> Making up a *sentence* in which the first letter of each word is also the initial letter of each item in the list you want to remember. For instance, supposing that you want a mnemonic for remembering metric measures: kilometre, hectometre, decametre, metre, decimetre, centimetre, millimetre. You could compile a sentence such as:

> *K*nights *h*ate *d*irty *m*en *d*eceiving *c*harming *m*aidens.

Rote learning

Try to make your mnemonics vivid, funny, absurd, vulgar.

(d) Rote learning is perhaps the lowest order of fixing in the memory. The secret of rote learning lies in constant *repetition* of the material: by writing it down, saying it out loud, singing it in the bath. Jot down what you wish to learn on small cards; keep them in your pocket and use any odd minute to go over the facts again and again and again.

If you positively seek to *deepen your understanding* of your material and to *reinforce your powers of recall*, you will be equipping yourself with insights and skills which will promote successful study and enrich your future life.

11. *Examinations*

Examinations are an inevitable part of most courses of study, but you should try not to become over-anxious about them. Remember that they are designed to allow students who were good enough to begin the course in the first place, and who have worked consistently and revised thoroughly, to do well. They are certainly *not* malicious attempts to thwart you or 'do you down'. It is also worth bearing in mind that if you have already completed to the best of your ability an examined coursework component, you are well on the road to success.

If a hard-working and conscientious student fails to do justice to himself in an examination, the fault will almost certainly lie in poor preparation or inadequate examination technique. The key to success lies in the acquisition and application over a period of time of effective revision techniques.

(1) Timing of Revision

You must remember that *you need to start revision early*. Intensive pre-examination revision, as distinct from normal course work revision, should cover a period of approximately eight weeks before the examination. Therefore, some two months before the examination you should draw up a schedule of revision and preparation which will take you through to the day of your final examination. Use your pad of study schedule sheets to draw up this scheme; block out timetabled periods and your 'recreation allowance', and you will be left with a reassuring prediction *well in advance* of the effective total revision time available.

The next step, as with planning your weekly schedule, is to

The equations on the blackboard:

$$\frac{s}{t} = \frac{u+v}{2}$$

$$\therefore \; s = \frac{1}{2}(u+v)t$$

$$\text{But} \quad v = u+at$$

$$\therefore \; s = \frac{1}{2}(u+u+at)$$

$$\text{or} \quad s = ut + \frac{1}{2}at^2$$

You need to start revision early

compile a complete list of *all* topics and materials to be revised. Many of these will arise naturally from coursework essays and other written projects; however, you will need to study the syllabus again, look closely at past examination papers – of which you must have copies – and check with fellow-students that you have not omitted anything of importance. It is a good idea to ask subject staff to check your topic list.

You are now in a position to begin completing the details of your schedule.

First, write in each examination, with its exact time and duration clearly shown. Next, begin to mark in your revision sessions, inserting topics from your master list. Limit each session to the standard time block, and remember that you must make provision for *regular review sessions of topics already covered*. In any one session of several hours, aim for a 'mix' of subjects so as to avoid boredom or falling into a rut. Allow yourself a brief coffee break between each block of revision, but do not allow this to encroach onto your schedule.

(2) Revision Technique

'Revision' is probably one of the most abused and misunderstood terms in education. For many students it seems to mean little more than a tortured and frustrated re-reading of old material, a passive and miserable staring at books and notes. The most valuable form of revision, however, is *totally and energetically active*, as will be seen shortly.

As already indicated, revision is not simply a pre-examination ritual, but should be an integral part of every student's approach throughout the course; re-reading, re-writing and amplification of notes, preparing for essays and daily checking of material just covered, all represent essential aspects of continuous revision.

Revision for examinations, however, is a more focused and specialised form of the technique. Literally, revision means 'seeing again', refreshing one's knowledge of and insight into important material.

The following points are central to effective revision technique:

(a) Your revision should be based largely on your notes, corrected essays and past examination papers. The final run-up to an examination is not the time to begin reading new books or working at fresh material. Past papers are particularly important to help you gain familiarity with the format of the examination.

(b) Aimless and generalised re-reading is not revision. The stress must be on *reorganisation and recall* rather than on simple reading. You must practise *doing* what the examination will require you to do, that is actively manipulating your material rather than simply pondering over it.

(c) The examination may very well require you to restructure your ideas and consider your material in a different light, in other words to *reorganise your knowledge*. In preparation, therefore, you should *re-arrange and summarise your material*, in the form of brief essay plans or abbreviated lists. Major topics should be reduced to one side of A4 containing important points, facts and ideas by no later than the week before the examination. Do this also for your essays. One side of paper – never write on both sides for revision purposes – should contain an outline of all the essential points needed to give a full answer. The very act of summarising and abbreviating your material will lodge it more firmly in your mind. Consider the value of doing a brief plan for any question that might come up. Always have rough paper at your side to jot down salient points as they occur to you. Read your plans and lists over and over again. Test yourself and get your family to help. *Learn and review* (Chapter 10).

(d) Revise all material on a particular topic at the same time.

(e) Work through a full past paper – in self-imposed examination conditions – at least once during your period of revision.

(f) Do not place too much faith in tactical 'spotting' of some questions while leaving other areas uncovered. You may well have certain favourite topics on which you wish to place special emphasis, but do not take the risk of ignoring significant areas.

(g) Do not be seduced by commercial 'cribs': books of examination notes, guides to set texts and so on. Whilst the best of these may be helpful if incorporated into a thorough and balanced schedule, undue reliance on them will lead you into the *passive* form of revision instead of the vital *active* variety.

(h) If any of your examinations are based on the 'open book' approach (particularly common in literature papers), this does not mean that you can go correspondingly easy on revision in this subject. On the contrary, you need to be just as much master of your material as would be required in the more conventional examining situation. In fact, having the book with you in the exam hall can be a positive disadvantage if you are not thoroughly familiar with it; thumbing feverishly through a half-learned text while the hands of the clock move round is not a sensible use of examination time.

(i) If you have a lot of diagrams or figures to revise, it may be useful to gather them together in several revision sheets, each containing a number of diagrams. Take photocopies of each sheet before you do any labelling. One copy of each sheet should then be fully labelled and have all the necessary detail added; the unlabelled copies will be valuable for revision purposes, for you can test yourself by labelling and adding detail from memory before checking against the 'master copy'.

(j) If you are doing any multiple-choice papers, you must practise the necessary techniques during your revision period. Buy copies of past papers from the examining board, and search out the collections of papers – covering several disciplines – which are now available in paperback; the latter are particularly useful because they usually have answers at the back, thus enabling you to assess your own performance.

(k) The physical circumstances of your revision should be conducive to hard work and undisturbed concentration; look again at the guide-lines in Chapter 3.

(3) The Day Before

Check the location of the examination hall and the starting time. Ensure also that your equipment is in order: pens, pencils, sharpener, ink/cartridges, rubber, ruler, watch, drawing instruments, calculator. Have replacements for anything that may break or run out – including spare batteries.

By all means do some light revision – final checking of brief plans, lists and so on – but do not do anything too intensive and certainly *do not look at anything new*.

Go to bed early and set the alarm so as to give you plenty of time in the morning. Ask someone at home to check that you have woken up. A cup of tea is always a help!

(4) The Moment Approaches

Avoid frenzied last minute checking of material and those ghoulish groups of fellow-examinees bent on mutual intimidation.

(5) In the Examination Hall

Ensure that you are fully and accurately aware of the centre number and of your candidate number.

Synchronise your watch and the examination hall clock; place your watch in front of you. Ask for enough sheets of paper to see you through the whole examination (plus one sheet for planning essays), so as to avoid having to disturb your concentration by asking for more.

(6) The Paper

(a) Read the rubric (italic instructions) *very carefully*. If you doubt the importance of this, have a look at the following:

Read the paper through once before answering the questions.
Write your answers on a separate sheet of paper.
Time allowed – fifteen minutes.

(i)	What is your name?
(ii)	What is your home address?
(iii)	What is today's date?
(iv)	What is the current rate of inflation?
(v)	What is the present level of unemployment in the UK?
(vi)	Who owns Times Newspapers Ltd?
(vii)	Who is the President of France?
(viii)	Which football team won the FA Cup last year?
(ix)	Which of these colours are primary ones – green, yellow, black, blue, mauve or red?
(x)	Who wrote *Barnaby Rudge*?
(xi)	How many countries are members of the EEC?
(xii)	How far is it from Manchester to Liverpool?
(xiii)	Who won the men's singles at Wimbledon last year?
(xiv)	What percentage of fat to flour is usually found in shortcrust pastry?

(xv)   What do the following knitting abbreviations stand for –
        K1, P1, K2tog, yfwd?

(xvi)   Which of the following are saints' names – Gillian,
        Benjamin, Eleanor, Matthew, Jonathan?

(xvii) Answer only the first three questions of this paper.

(xviii) What is your favourite colour?

(xix)   What is the meaning of life?

(xx)   What will the weather be like tomorrow?

You will see that the detailed instructions are crucial!

Many candidates seriously damage their chances by answering the
wrong number of questions. If you answer too few, the danger is
obvious. Answer too many, and the extra ones will be ignored; the
marker will *not* hunt through to select the best ones. You will have
wasted time which could well have improved the quality of the
questions which *are* counted.

(b) Concentrate on the key issues:
    How many questions to be done?
    Are any compulsory?
    In answer booklets or on paper?
    Should each answer begin on a fresh sheet?

(c) You must first read right through the whole paper and consider all of the questions. If you have a choice, tick those you think
you can do as you go along. If some sub-sections of a particular
question have more marks allocated to them than other sub-
sections, circle these.
    Re-read the questions you have ticked. Note carefully the phras-
ing; check the *key words*. Then make your final selection which you
will show by ticking twice, taking care not to be carried away by
your ambition; it is better to make a good job of a straightforward
question than to do less well at a more demanding one.

(d) Now that you have decided which questions to do, there are two possible approaches:

    (i)   Deal with the questions one by one, with five minutes planning before each; this is probably the most common approach.

    (ii)   Prepare plans for all of your answers at the beginning of the examination; this may have the advantage of giving you in advance a reassuring awareness that you are going to be able to cope with the whole paper.

(e) After this preliminary work you must construct a timetable for yourself; divide the number of questions to be completed into the amount of time left, then establish the deadlines to which you must adhere, for example first question done by 10.05 and so on. Do all in your power to keep to these deadlines and try to make provision for a fifteen minute checking session at the end.

(f) If you have a choice, start with the question about which you are most confident. Remember your essay writing technique and guide-lines on diagrams, graphs and tables. Ensure that you are always answering the question. Check briefly after each one.

(g) Some points on lay-out:

    (i)   Many subjects require 'working out' to be shown. Make sure that you meet such requirements in clear and legible style. Accurate working out will often gain marks even when there are mistakes in the substance of the answer.

    (ii)   Initial planning should be shown, ruled off when completed and crossed through with a single neat stroke. Such preliminary work may well persuade the examiner to the view that he is dealing with an orderly and analytical individual!

    (iii)   If a question is divided into numbered and lettered subsections, make sure that your answer corresponds to this pattern.

(iv) Do not encroach on the margins.

(v) Use plenty of paper. Be spacious in your lay-out; this will make your paper easier for the examiner to mark, and will offer you scope for later additions and amendments during your final check.

(h) Do all in your power to avoid the following basic mistakes:

(i) Simply ignoring the question asked. Many candidates insist on writing a prepared answer which they have memorised – or one on an associated topic more to their taste – and either fail completely to answer the question, or make only brief reference to it at the beginning or end.

(ii) Twisting the question so that it roughly fits a prepared essay, line of thought or collection of quotations. Many candidates seem to think that something fairly close to the question will do.

(iii) Partial irrelevance: starting on the point, but wandering away from it.

(iv) Irrelevance through what has been called 'saturation bombing'; this is a method much favoured by those candidates determined to write down all they know on a particular subject, instead of tailoring their material *selectively* to the question.

(v) Irrelevance through simple narrative. Considerable numbers of candidates opt for a straight – and fatal – recital of events, without the *comment and analysis* that are so crucial.

(i) It is *vital* to finish the required number of questions, otherwise you are not going to be marked out of the maximum. Another way of considering this: if you have to do five questions, you will probably need to score an average of eight out of twenty in order to pass. Complete only three questions, and you will need to be scoring fourteen out of twenty on each – a very different proposition!

If you seriously miscalculate the time, remember that it is worthwhile to aim for an outline plan of your final answer.

If you run out of ideas on a particular answer, leave a suitable space for completion later on and move to another question. Do not sit and agonise while time passes.

(j) A final check through the whole paper is essential. No matter how unappealing a prospect, you must read every word you have written. Further points and additional information may have occurred to you, which can now be added – hence the usefulness of a 'spacious' approach to the setting out of your answers. This is also the time to finish off questions on which you may have 'run dry' earlier. Crucially, this final checking period enables you to spot basic errors, slips of the pen, miscalculations, misquotations and so on; this can often make a difference of 5 to 10 per cent.

(7) Multiple Choice Papers

This method of examining – common in many subject areas – is regarded by some authorities as superior to traditional approaches in that it tests 'pure knowledge' only; in other words it assesses simply what a candidate knows, and makes no additional demands on his ability to write continuous prose, plan essays, draw shapes and figures or design charts and diagrams.

The basic approach is always the same; the question is followed by a list consisting of a correct answer and several plausible, though incorrect, alternatives (known in the business as 'distractors'). It is the candidate's task to select the correct alternative, normally by entering a simple mark on an answer sheet.

Thus, multiple choice examining seems in many ways to be the answer to a student's prayer; there is no essay technique or structured exposition to cope with, and you *know* that the correct answer is down there somewhere, albeit cunningly fenced about with false alternatives. Marks, it would appear, are there to be scored quickly and directly.

It is, of course, a far more demanding situation than this, and you would do well to consider the following points:

(a) The apparent simplicity of the multiple choice format in itself poses a problem. Because they have very little actually to *write*, many students tend to rush through the paper with wild abandon. This is a grave mistake; the distractors are designed to be realistic and credible, and will certainly be likely to catch out anybody who is not concentrating. In general, it is the weaker candidates who rush through; the more able take their time and spend longer on considering the differentiations involved.

(b) Multiple choice questions are not restricted to simple fact-based responses. This mode of examining is perfectly capable of calling for deduction, evaluation and interpretation of data. The swiftness with which a response may be made often diverts attention from the thought that should go into it.

(c) Multiple choice questions can be, and usually are, varied in format. The following approaches are typical:

(i)   Four or five straight alternatives, with only one correct answer.

(ii)   Multiple completion: in this case, *combinations* of alternatives may need to be considered, for example:
Select A if 1, 2 and 3 are correct
      B if 1 and 2 only are correct
      C if 2 and 3 only are correct

(iii)   Matching pairs: here there may be a choice of four or five definitions or descriptions, with the candidate required to select the one matching the term in the question.

(iv)   Sentence/paragraph completion: in this situation there is often a short passage with some words missing. The candidate has to select alternatives from a list to fill the gaps.

You will see that the multiple-choice format is more complex than might at first be imagined.

(d) Because of the nature of the multiple choice approach, a single examination paper may contain a great volume of questioning. You will need to know the syllabus well!

(e) We are dealing here with an 'all or nothing' situation. Although it is clearly possible to pick up marks by luck or guesswork, it is equally true that if you select the wrong alternative you get nothing. This is not always the case in traditional papers, where an incorrect answer may still attract some marks for its general presentation, trend of thought or working out.

(f) Tactics

(i) Read carefully through the whole paper before you begin answering the questions.

(ii) Divide up the remaining time between sections and questions, just as you would on an essay paper.

(iii) Now begin answering. There are two basic techniques of identifying the correct alternatives:

● Immediate recognition
● Elimination of the distractors so as to isolate the correct option.

The first approach is obviously the faster of the two, and quite permissible if you are *absolutely certain* of your choice. If there is any degree of doubt or uncertainty, it is a good practice to make a double-check by using both methods on each question.

(iv) Use rough paper to sketch out your ideas and clarify your thinking. There is no less need for thoughtful preparation simply because the process of entering the answers is so straightforward.

(v) If you are quite baffled, *guess*. You should never leave a question unanswered.

(vi) Check very carefully for slips of the pen; this kind of inaccuracy is obviously a real problem in multiple choice examinations, where circling the wrong number or shading the wrong box will lose you *all* of the marks available. If you make an alteration, ensure that your new choice is perfectly clear.

Blissful Release!

When you leave the examination hall, it is best not to wait around for morbid discussions with fellow-students. Mutual interrogation is likely to leave you feeling unsettled about your performance. Much better to go home for a rest or out for a walk.

Appendix 1: A Hundred of the Best: A Leisure Reading List

The list which follows is of necessity highly selective and very much a matter of the author's personal choice. None the less, it does include many great novelists, as well as several compelling writers of lesser rank. In general, even with the 'classics', only one work per author is listed; the hope is that a first acquaintance will lead you on to seek for more. A series of linked novels is counted as one entry.

Acquire as many as possible of these titles, most of them available in paperback, and you will have the nucleus of a fine personal library.

The Classics

Austen, Jane (1775–1817) — *Pride and Prejudice* (Penguin)
Brontë, Charlotte (1816–1855) — *Jane Eyre* (Penguin)
Brontë, Emily (1818–1848) — *Wuthering Heights* (Penguin)
Conrad, Joseph (1857–1924) — *The Secret Agent* (Penguin)
Dickens, Charles (1812–1870) — *Bleak House* (Penguin)
Eliot, George (1819–1880) — *Middlemarch* (Penguin)
Hardy, Thomas (1840–1928) — *Far From the Madding Crowd* (Macmillan)

James, Henry (1843–1916) — *The Portrait of a Lady* (Penguin)
Thackeray, William (1811–1863) — *Vanity Fair* (Penguin)
Trollope, Anthony (1815–1882) — *Barchester Towers* (Dent/Everyman)

Historical Narratives

Du Maurier, Daphne — *Jamaica Inn* (Pan)

Fowles, John	*The French Lieutenant's Woman* (Panther)
Graves, Robert	*I, Claudius* (Penguin)
Nye, Robert	*Falstaff* (Sphere)
Renault, Mary	*The Bull from the Sea* (Penguin)
Stone, Irving	*The Agony and the Ecstasy* (Collins)

The Twentieth Century Perspective

Baldwin, James	*Another Country* (Corgi)
Barstow, Stan	*A Kind of Loving* (Corgi)
Bellow, Saul	*The Adventures of Augie March* (Penguin)
Bradbury, Malcolm	*The History Man* (Arrow)
Donleavy, J. P.	*The Ginger Man* (Penguin)
Durrell, Lawrence	*The Alexandria Quartet* (series) (Faber)
Fitzgerald, Scott	*The Great Gatsby* (Penguin)
Forster, E. M.	*A Passage to India* (Penguin)
Golding, William	*Lord of the Flies* (Faber)
Greene, Graham	*The Power and the Glory* (Penguin)
Greenwood, Walter	*Love on the Dole* (Penguin)
Hartley, L. P.	*The Go-Between* (Penguin)
Hemingway, Ernest	*A Farewell to Arms* (Panther)
Joyce, James	*Ulysses* (Penguin)
Lawrence, D. H.	*Sons and Lovers* (Penguin)
Lee, Harper	*To Kill a Mockingbird* (Pan)
Llewellyn, Richard	*How Green was my Valley* (New English Library)
Malamud, Bernard	*The Fixer* (Penguin)
Moore, Brian	*Catholics* (Penguin)
Murdoch, Iris	*The Bell* (Panther)
O'Brien, Edna	*The Country Girls* (Penguin)
Orwell, George	*Animal Farm* (Penguin)
Pasternak, Boris	*Doctor Zhivago* (Fontana)
Paton, Alan	*Cry, The Beloved Country* (Penguin)
Plunkett, James	*Strumpet City* (Arrow)
Powell, Anthony	*A Dance to the Music of Time* (series) (Fontana)
Salinger, J. D.	*The Catcher in the Rye* (Penguin)
Scott, Paul	*The Raj Quartet* (series) (Panther)
Sillitoe, Alan	*Saturday Night and Sunday Morning* (Star)
Snow, C. P.	*Strangers and Brothers* (series) (Penguin)
Solzhenitzyn, Alexander	*Cancer Ward* (Penguin)
Spring, Howard	*Fame is the Spur* (Fontana)
Steinbeck, John	*The Grapes of Wrath* (Pan)

A Hundred of the Best: A Leisure Reading List

Waugh, Evelyn	*Brideshead Revisited* (Penguin)
Wilson, Angus	*Anglo-Saxon Attitudes* (Penguin)
Woolf, Virginia	*To the Lighthouse* (Panther)

Autobiography/Social Documentary

Blythe, Ronald	*Akenfield: Portrait of an English Village* (Penguin)
Joyce, James	*A Portrait of the Artist as a Young Man* (Panther)
Lee, Laurie	*Cider with Rosie* (Penguin)
Thompson, Flora	*Lark Rise to Candleford* (Penguin)

Crime/Thriller

Chandler, Raymond	*Farewell My Lovely* (Penguin)
Christie, Agatha	*Murder on the Orient Express* (Fontana)
James, P. D.	*Cover Her Face* (Sphere)
Sayers, Dorothy	*The Nine Tailors* (New English Library)
Tey, Josephine	*The Daughter of Time* (Penguin)

Espionage

Childers, Erskine	*The Riddle of the Sands* (Dover)
Deighton, Len	*The Ipcress File* (Panther)
Fleming, Ian	*Goldfinger* (Panther)
Forsyth, Frederick	*The Devil's Alternative* (Corgi)
Le Carré, John	*The Spy Who Came In From The Cold* (Pan)

War

(a) Fiction

Deighton, Len	*Bomber* (Panther)
Heller, Joseph	*Catch 22* (Corgi)
Johnston, Jennifer	*How Many Miles to Babylon?* (Coronet)
Keneally, Thomas	*Schindler's Ark* (Coronet)
Mailer, Norman	*The Naked and the Dead* (Panther)
Monsarrat, Nicholas	*The Cruel Sea* (Penguin)
Remarque, Erich Maria	*All Quiet on the Western Front* (Mayflower)
Shute, Nevil	*A Town Like Alice* (Pan)

(b) Real-life

Graves, Robert	*Goodbye to All That* (Penguin)
Hersey, John	*Hiroshima* (Penguin)
Neave, Airey	*They Have Their Exits* (Hodder)

Animal Stories

(a) Fiction

Adams, Richard	*Watership Down* (Penguin)
Bach, Richard	*Jonathan Livingston Seagull* (Pan)

(b) Real-life

Durrell, Gerald	*Zoo in my Luggage* (Penguin)
Maxwell, Gavin	*Ring of Bright Water* (Penguin)
Williamson, Henry	*Tarka the Otter* (Penguin)

Humour

Amis, Kingsley	*Lucky Jim* (Penguin)
Coren, Alan	*The Sanity Inspector* (Coronet)
Thurber, James	*The Beast in Me and Other Animals* (Penguin)
Wodehouse, P. G.	*Jeeves and the Feudal Spirit* (Coronet)

Fantasy, Myth, Legend

Fowles, John	*The Magus* (Panther)
Golding, William	*The Spire* (Faber)
Hoban, Russell	*Riddley Walker* (Pan)
James, M. R.	*Ghost Stories* (Arnold)
Peake, Mervyn	*The Gormenghast Trilogy* (Penguin)
Poe, Edgar Allan	*Tales of Mystery and Imagination* (Pan)
Tolkien, J. R. R.	*The Lord of the Rings* (Allen & Unwin)

Science Fiction

Aldiss, Brian	*Canopy of Time* (New English Library)
Asimov, Isaac	*Fantastic Voyage* (Corgi)
Bradbury, Ray	*Golden Apples of the Sun* (Panther)
Clarke, Arthur C.	*2001: A Space Odyssey* (Arrow)
Herbert, Frank	*Dune* (New English Library)
Smith, E. E. 'Doc'	*Children of the Lens* (Panther)
Wyndham, John	*The Midwich Cuckoos* (Penguin)

Appendix 2: Reference Books

Please note that the following list is only a very small selection and that many famous works of reference are omitted. None the less, it should give you an indication of the range of resources available and of how there is usually a reference book for every need, either general or specialist.

General

Oxford English Dictionary	Thirteen volumes. Somewhat outdated, but good on derivations and variety of meaning.
Chambers Twentieth Century Dictionary	Splendid single-volume work.
Dictionary of Slang and Unconventional English	(Partridge) Words and phrases not often found in dictionaries! (Routledge & Kegan Paul)
Roget's Thesaurus	Marvellous help when you can't think of the *exact* word you are seeking. Words grouped according to meaning. (Several publishers, including Longman and Penguin)
Oxford Dictionary of Quotations	Fascinating and comprehensive selection.
Brewer's Dictionary of Phrase and Fable	Compelling store-house of definitions, references, origins of phrases, mythological background. (Cassell)
Pears Cyclopaedia	Superb annual. Reviews events of history and the past year. Range of varied and authoritative specialist sections. (Pelham Books)

Whitaker's Almanac	Annual publication: official statistics, addresses. Mine of information, essential data and dates for the year ahead.
Encyclopaedia Britannica	Thirty volumes, sub-divided into three sections:

(a) A one-volume 'Propaedia', which is a guide to the set and an outline of knowledge in various fields.

(b) A ten-volume 'Micropaedia' which acts as an extensive 'ready reference section'.

(c) A nineteen-volume 'Macropaedia' which studies subjects in great depth.

The set is updated annually with a 'Book of the Year'.

Macmillan Encyclopaedia	Attractive and comprehensive single volume.

Specialist

Fontana Dictionary of Modern Thought	Concepts, technical terms, -ism. (Collins)
Illustrated Dictionary of World Religions	Brief, clear and helpful. (Religious Education Press)
Annual Abstract of Statistics	Official statistical details of virtually all aspects of the social, economic and industrial life of the country. (HMSO)
Britain 19..	Annual. Established work of reference: factual and statistical information on government and other institutions. (HMSO)
Statesman's Yearbook	Annual. Countries of the world, official data, currencies, descriptions and so on. (Macmillan)
Dod's Parliamentary Companion	Tiny annual. Guide to MPs, various posts and traditions in Parliament.
Keesing's Contemporary Archives	Meticulous and continuously updated record of current events. (Longman)
Dictionary of Modern Economics	25,000 entries. Up-to-date, authoritative. (Macmillan)

A Dictionary of the Law	Comprehensive work. (Macdonald & Evans)
Everyman's Own Lawyer	Digest of the law, written in layman's language: simply arranged. (Macmillan)
Encyclopaedia of Mathematics	Accurate and attractive work. Huge amount of information. (Prentice Hall)
A Dictionary of Statistical Terms	Authoritative work. (Longman)
Chambers Dictionary of Science and Technology	Standard work.
McGraw-Hill Encyclopaedia of Science and Technology	Huge work (fifteen volumes). Detailed and comprehensive.
New Larousse Encyclopaedia of Animal Life	Beautifully illustrated work of reference.
Dictionary of Computing	Comprehensive and up-to-date (Oxford)
Black's Medical Dictionary	Standard work.
Trade Directories (e.g. Kelly's)	Vast volumes which detail companies, businesses and addresses in UK and internationally.
Who Owns Whom	Annual. Details of company structures and associations. (Dunn & Bradstreet)
Business Terms, Phrases and Abbreviations	Standard work. (Pitman)
International Dictionary of Management	Extremely useful compendium of key words and phrases. (Kogan Page)
Penguin Dictionary of Commerce	A simple and concise handbook.
A Biographical Dictionary of Artists	Superbly illustrated work of reference. (Macmillan)
Dictionary of Art Terms and Techniques	(Mayer) Broad and useful coverage. (Black)
A Dictionary of Architecture	Scholarly work by Pevsner et al. (Penguin)
The Oxford Companion to Art	Clear and concise work of reference.
A Dictionary of Musical Themes	Every important theme in classical music. (Faber)
Groves Dictionary of Music and Musicians	*The* work of reference. Multi-volume.

Oxford Companion to Music	Helpful and comprehensive.
Official Rules of Sports and Games	Standard reference work. (Kaye & Ward)
Oxford Companion to Sports and Games	Fascinatingly complete and well illustrated
Oxford Companion to English Literature	Standard work. Literary figures, works, plot summaries and so on. NB Other volumes in the series cover the literature of many modern and classical languages.
Oxford Companion to the Theatre	Mass of detail on plays, actors, performance, technical aspects.
Everyman's Companion to Shakespeare	Thematic arrangement. Glossary, plot summaries. Mine of fascinating information. (Dent)
The Cambridge Ancient History	Multi-volume sets. Weighty and authoritative.
The Cambridge Medieval History	
The New Cambridge Modern History	
Encyclopaedia of Dates and Events	Chronological outline survey (from pre-history to 1970s) of man's achievements in history, literature, arts and science. (Teach Yourself Books, Hodder and Stoughton)
Macmillan Dictionary of Archaeology	Comprehensive work.
A Dictionary of British History	Splendid work of reference from the Roman period to 1970 (Secker & Warburg)
Dictionary of National Biography	Biographies of all figures of national importance. Began in 1885: now published and updated by Oxford. Runs to more than 70 volumes.
Macmillan Dictionary of Biography	Single-volume coverage of prominent people from all ages and nations.
The Times Atlas of the World (Comprehensive Edition)	Magnificent single-volume work.
Glossary of Geographical Terms	Clear and helpful definitions. (Longman)
Meteorological Glossary	Official work of reference. (HMSO)

Appendix 3: Newspapers and Periodicals

All students should aim to keep themselves well informed about current events and issues, so that they can participate in discussion in an informed manner. This will be a particularly valuable asset when you attend interviews for higher education or employment. Knowledge of current affairs can be obtained from two main sources:
  (a) Radio and television
  (b) Newspapers and weekly magazines

(a) *Radio and Television*

You should certainly listen each day to at least one extended news broadcast. A good combination would include breakfast-time radio coverage (*not* on a popular music channel) and one of the late-evening news programmes on television. Try to develop a *continuity* of interest in a variety of main items; see how they develop across a period of time. Do attempt to avoid the prejudiced 'deaf ear'; it *is* important to keep up-to-date with foreign affairs and finance, as well as with domestic items of more immediate appeal.

Apart from news bulletins, you should also watch regularly some of the excellent television documentaries on current affairs.

(b) *Newspapers and Weekly Magazines*

Popular newspapers tend to provide only superficial coverage of news events and concentrate on the sensational to the detriment of the serious. Included in this category are: *The Daily Mail, The Daily Mirror, The Daily Express, The Sun, The Star* and their Sunday equivalents.

Quality newspapers are of far more value to the serious student, and you would be well advised to subscribe to one of them, if you do not already do so. These include:

- *The Daily Telegraph* – very full news and sports coverage, though somewhat lacking in discursive articles and features: staunchly Tory.

- *The Guardian* – excellent articles: lively coverage of arts and political events: fine book reviews: Liberal Democrat political stance.

- *The Times* – full and serious coverage: useful articles: authoritative and comprehensive.

- *The Independent* – sane, balanced and strictly without any political affiliation.

- *The Sunday Telegraph* – as for *The Daily Telegraph*.

- *The Observer* – wide ranging coverage of domestic and international affairs: liberal political stance.

- *The Sunday Times* – lively, in-depth analysis: good book reviews: full and wide-ranging coverage.

Weekly magazines – if you do not wish to purchase, these may be consulted in most school, college and public libraries. All those listed below are well presented, detailed, and often contain excellent articles, book reviews and short essays. Try to find time each week to look through them, both for general interest and for information relevant to your academic study. You may wish to take notes from some of the more useful articles.

These magazines include:

- *The Economist*: weekly current affairs analysis.

- *Newsweek*: international news coverage.

- *Time*: high-quality production: fine photo-journalism.

● *New Scientist*: up-to-date and wide-ranging.

Also available in many libraries are a number of specialist journals which may, however, be of general interest, for example *Geographical Magazine*, *History Today* and so on.

Do not underestimate the importance of your local newspaper, which provides an important insight into local government, planning issues and matters concerning the environment.

Appendix 4: A Student's Glossary

The purpose of this glossary is to give brief and simple definitions of words, phrases and names which may prove confusing to some students. Because the structure of public examinations is continuously evolving, no attempt has been made to include the names of specific examinations or examining boards. It should also be noted that during the first half of the 1990s, the 'binary divide' between universities and polytechnics is being removed. This will allow polytechnics to award their own degrees and, if they so wish, to assume the title of university.

Sectors and Institutions

Further Education (FE)	Includes all provision in post-16 education, except degree courses, Higher National Diploma, Diploma in HE, etc. Much of FE is vocationally based, though not exclusively so.
Higher Education (HE)	The university/institute sector, where courses result in the award of a degree, diploma or other advanced qualification.
Adult Education	A wide range of training and education provided most often in institutions other than those attended by school leavers. Ranges from short, interest/recreation-based courses to first degree level and beyond.
Sixth-Form College	An institution which caters both for the traditional sixth-former and for the less academic student. All of the options found in school sixth-forms are on offer, together with a variety of other courses.

Tertiary College	Institution providing all of the post–16 education in a particular area, both full and part time. Combines the normal range of sixth-form courses with the vocational and technical courses associated with colleges of FE.
College of Further Education	A college serving its own locality and providing a range of academic and vocational courses. The majority of students are in the 16–19 age group.
Polytechnic	A term now falling into disuse, as polytechnics assume the status and name of University. Often enjoying strong links with local industry and business, polytechnics/new universities offer a wide range of courses – full, part-time and sandwich – in technology, science and the arts. Many of the courses are at degree level, though some of the most significant are at the level of advanced diplomas.
College of Education	Institution offering teacher training to the level of B. Ed. May be denominational. Greatly reduced in number in the 1970s. Many merged with polytechnics and colleges of FE: others combined to produce institutes/colleges of HE (see below).
Institute/College of Higher Education	Often arose from the amalgamation of colleges of education. Not restricted to producing teachers; degree courses are offered in teacher education, humanities and sciences, as well as diplomas in HE.

Applying for a Place

Prospectus	A descriptive guide to an institution, giving details of staff, resources, courses offered.
UCCA/PCAS/UCAS	Universities Central Council on Admissions/Polytechnic Central Admissions System. The clearing-house procedures through which all applications for entrance must pass. To be replaced by a unified system (UCAS) as the 'binary divide' between university and polytechnic disappears.

Appendix 4

Financial Support

Mandatory Award
: A grant which an LEA is required *by law* to make to a full-time student undertaking a recognised advanced course. Covers fees and maintenance.

Discretionary Award
: A grant which an LEA *may* make if it so decides. Usually for courses below degree level; a typical example would be an award to a 16-18 student from a needy family in order to allow attendance at the local college of FE.

Bursary
: An award made by a firm, company, college or other institution to subsidise and support a student during his course of study.

Sponsorship
: Most commonly, an arrangement whereby a firm or company selects a promising student for future employment, supplementing his grant with a 'salary' while he is training.

Administrative Staff

Registrar
: A post of senior rank in a college or university. The registrar is responsible for student registration, record-keeping, examinations and general administration.

Bursar
: A senior post in a school or college, whose holder is responsible for finance and maintenance of buildings.

Vice-Chancellor
: The senior-ranking academic and administrative officer of a university.

Chancellor
: The nominal head of a university: normally present only on ceremonial occasions.

Teaching Staff

Don
: A term originally applied only to Fellows of Oxford and Cambridge, it now is used of university teachers in general.

Fellow

(a) A senior member of an Oxford or Cambridge college, with administrative and teaching responsibilities.

(b) A member of a learned body or professional group.

(c) A fellow may also be a member of a college or university who is engaged in research supported by special funds.

Assistant Lecturer

The lowest rank in the college or university teaching order, which then proceeds through Lecturer, Senior Lecturer, Principal Lecturer and Reader to the level of Professor, who is a university's highest ranking teacher in a particular subject. A professor may occupy a specified post, for instance the 'Chair' of a specific subject. Alternatively, the term 'Professor' may be a recognition simply of outstanding academic merit.

Course Structure

Tripos

An honours degree course at Cambridge. Two Tripos examinations must be passed for a BA, though they need not be in the same subject area.

Foundation Course

An introductory course designed to provide a basis for a more advanced programme of study.

Common Core

Most commonly found in schools, this term refers to that part of the curriculum which *every student* must study.

Options/Elective Subjects

Subjects which a student *chooses* to study.

Subsidiary Subjects

Subjects studied at a lower level and for less time than the main subject. A student on a typical honours degree course might be expected to study two subsidiary subjects.

Modular

Refers to the sort of course where a student – instead of studying one subject in great depth – selects 'modules' or components of study from several

	different subject areas in order to meet his own needs and tastes more closely.
Credit	A 'point' which is awarded upon successful completion of a course or module, and which contributes to a designated total of credits required for a particular qualification.
Curriculum	In its most basic sense, this term refers to the *whole* programme of instruction, in all subjects and at all levels, offered in a school or other institution.
Syllabus	An outline of the areas to be covered in a single subject or a specific course.
Discipline	A specific subject or area of knowledge.
Inter-disciplinary	Refers to an approach in which two or more subjects are studied together, each focusing upon common areas so as to cross-fertilise and interact in a planned and co-ordinated way.
Multi-disciplinary	Less structured and harmonised than inter-disciplinary, this refers to an approach in which several subject areas are studied, perhaps identifying a common topic, but treating it very much from their own point of view.
Humanities	An umbrella term used to group together those subjects primarily concerned with the study of some aspect of human life and society. Obvious members of this group are history, human geography, religion, philosophy and the social sciences; the study of language and literature is often also included.
Liberal Studies	An area of the curriculum in colleges, designed to off-set the narrowing effects of strictly vocational study. Typical areas covered might include the cinema, literature and social studies.
Faculty	A large sub-division in a school, college or university, grouping together subjects and staff from a range of allied disciplines.
Vocational Courses	Courses of education or training aimed at teaching the practical skills and theory of a specific trade or occupation.

Linked Course	A course operated (and usually staffed) jointly by two or more institutions. A typical link would be between a school and its local college of FE.
Day Release	An arrangement whereby an employee is 'released' for one or two days per week during term-time, in order to train and qualify in a skill appropriate to his employment.
Block Release	Similar in principle to the above, though the 'release' is for a much longer period of time (see Sandwich Course).
Sandwich Course	Increasingly popular in many polytechnics and some universities, sandwich courses combine periods of full-time study alternating with full-time employment. The sandwich may be 'thick' with full-time employment for as long as a year, or 'thin' embodying perhaps two or three periods of employment, each lasting for half a year.
Extra-mural	This term is used to describe a department of a college or university which arranges courses for the public at large, as part of the provision for adult education.

Books

Blurb	Publisher's jargon for the short publicity paragraph about the book and the author which often appears on the back cover of a paperback.
Foreword	One of the preliminary items in a book, in which an expert or figure of authority contributes an endorsement or recommendation either of book or author.
Preface	Opening remarks by the author himself.
Appendix	A supplement or addition to a book, containing matter which is relevant to the text, but not necessarily essential to its completeness.

Bibliography

A descriptive list at the end of a book, essay or article, which gives details (title, author, publisher, date and place of publication) of every book read or consulted by the writer.

Glossary

Most commonly, a list at the end of a book giving the meanings of any words or phrases (often technical) which might be expected to cause difficulty.

Index

An alphabetically arranged catalogue of subjects dealt with, located at the end of a book and giving page references of all items included.

ISBN

International Standard Book Number. A ten-digit code number which is unique to the book which carries it. Eliminates the need to quote title, author, edition and publisher in full. *British Books in Print* carries a full list of ISBNs.

The Teaching Context

Lecture

Most commonly used in FE and HE, this refers to a fairly large scale teaching situation, in which the lecturer talks at length on his topic to students who are expected to take notes. Often followed by smaller group reinforcement.

Tutorial

Small group teaching context commonly found in FE and HE, in which a tutor will meet with one or more students to discuss an essay or other piece of submitted work.

Seminar

This is most often taken to mean a group meeting of students and tutor, often for the purpose of closer examination of a topic covered in a lecture.

Your Own Writing

Project

Although this can refer to a large-scale research undertaking, it most often for students suggests the preparation of a 'long essay' on a subject of the student's

	own choice, and involving a good deal of independent work and gathering of material.
Dissertation	A substantial piece of work which is often a requirement for an award or qualification. Typical features may include a research element, or at least a careful gathering and sifting of material, a balanced and clear structure and a moderately expressed and coherent 'argument' or line of thought.
Thesis	This normally refers to a very demanding piece of individually prepared work, similar to a dissertation, but longer and more extensively researched.
Fieldwork	A (usually short) period of study spent away from school, college or university, in which the student engages in a good deal of practical work and 'writing up' of observations. Typical of subjects such as geography and biology.
Research	A careful and scholarly investigation or inquiry into a particular field, with a view to contributing to knowledge in that subject area or to arranging and re-structuring facts and material in a new and helpful way. The stress is on detailed examination and careful recording of sources.
Manuscript	A writer's original version of a text or essay – hand-written or typed, not printed (abbreviation MS).
Draft	A preliminary outline or first rough version of a piece of writing.
Plagiarism	The unauthorised and unacknowledged copying of another person's material, implying that it is one's own.
Verbatim	Word for word.

Psychological Terms

IQ	(Intelligence quotient). A measure of performance in a standardised intelligence

test. Average is 100. 75 per cent of the population would be expected to score between 85 and 115.

Mnemonic
An artificial 'memory jogging' device.

Convergent Thinking
A mode of thinking which focuses on only one approach to a problem or situation.

Divergent Thinking
A mode of thinking which casts around for a variety of solutions or approaches.

Lateral Thinking
Similar to divergent thinking. The approach is to look at an object or situation from many viewpoints.

Examinations and Tests

Aptitude Test
A test (often practical) designed to establish whether an individual has the potential to cope with the skills and demands of a particular occupation or course of training.

Attainment Test
A test designed to reveal the amount of knowledge already acquired in a particular area.

Continuous Assessment
A technique of grading a student's achievement by continuous measuring of performance throughout the course, rather than in a 'one-off' examination situation.

Profile
An attempt to move away from the traditional report or examination result, which deals only with performance in a particular subject. A profile aims to give a rounded and complete indication in an analytical way of the whole range of a student's talents, abilities, attitudes and behaviour.

Graded Tests
Instead of final examinations at the end of a five-year course at school, graded tests are designed to allow students to make progress and be assessed at their own pace. They can be taken at any time; if the pupil is successful, he moves on to the next stage or grade.

Multiple Choice Tests
A common approach to examining, in which the candidate is required to select

	the correct answer from a list which also includes several 'distractors' (similar, but incorrect answers).
Open-ended Tests	The opposite of the multiple-choice approach. Here the candidate is invited to express the answer in his own words.
Rubric	The crucial instructions to candidates included in all examination papers. Usually printed in italics.
Invigilator	An officially appointed person – often a member of the teaching staff – whose responsibility is to supervise students while they are taking their examination papers.
Scripts	Jargon for completed answer papers.
Oral	An examination situation – usually on a one-to-one basis – in which the candidate is judged on his *spoken* response to the examiner's questions.
Aural	An examination situation which seeks to measure candidate's *listening* skills; typically, the candidate listens to a taped or spoken passage and answers questions on its content.
Viva	Abbreviated form of 'viva voce'. An oral examination often set as part of the assessment for a higher degree.
Moderator	An official appointed by an examining body to supervise examinations where there is an element of school/college assessment. His responsibility is to ensure comparability of standards between the different institutions, often adjusting marks to compensate for undue leniency or severity.
Norm-Referenced Examination	A form of assessment in which a candidate's grade is decided on the basis of his performance compared with the performance of all other candidates.
Criterion-Referenced Examination	The opposite of norm referencing, this approach grades candidates according to a fixed standard or level of competence. The driving test is often quoted as an example of this principle.

129

Matriculation	Gaining the qualifications required for entry to an institution.
Diploma	A qualification dependent upon successful completion of a course of study. May be below degree level, or restricted to graduates. Many diplomas are awarded by professional bodies.
Honours Degree	The highest of the first level of degrees (see below). It involves study in depth of a major subject area. More demanding than a 'pass' degree, an honours degree is usually awarded in one of three classes, ranging from first (the highest) to third. The second class is often further divided into upper and lower.
External Degree	A degree which does not require the candidate's attendance at the awarding institution, but requires him to pass the appropriate examinations. A popular medium of study for external degrees is by correspondence course.
Honorary Degree	A 'ceremonial' degree – not dependent upon study or academic performance – awarded by an institution as a mark of recognition of a distinguished person's achievements.

Levels of Degrees

Bachelor	Nearly always a first degree, although this does not apply to some Scottish universities. Other exceptions are B Litt and B Phil, which are usually higher degrees. Bachelor degree courses normally last for three years.
Master	Most often a higher degree, awarded after one or two years of study, often including a component of research. In Scotland the MA is usually a first degree, while holders of a Bachelor's degree from Oxford or Cambridge may be awarded a Master's, upon payment of the appropriate fee, seven years after their first graduation.
Doctor	A doctorate is signified by the initials PhD or D Phil (Doctor of Philosophy). It is

awarded upon presentation and
acceptance of a substantial research thesis,
representing an original contribution to
knowledge in a particular area.

Miscellaneous

Campus
The grounds, buildings and entire estate
on which an educational institution is
situated.

Mature Student
For the purposes of grant awards, this
term is normally taken as referring to
students over the age of twenty-five.

Semester
Instead of dividing the academic year into
three terms, universities in the USA sub-
divide the year into two semesters, each
lasting approximately fifteen weeks.

Sabbatical
A period of leave – on full pay – for the
purpose of study or research. Normally
restricted to teachers in HE.

Index

Index